Nelson Thornes **Framework English**

Access
Skills in **Non-Fiction**

3

Wendy Wren
Series Consultant: **John Jackman**

Contents

Section	Text type	Word	Sentence	Writing	Page
Unit 1 Absolute power corrupts absolutely					
1 Gladiator – the movie	Film review	Vocabulary: dictionary and contextual work Spelling: 'aw' words	Noun and verb agreement	Information and opinion	4
2 Make the punishment fit the crime	Historical recount	Vocabulary: dictionary and contextual work Spelling: compound words	Alliteration	Recounts / autobiography	10
3 Marriage in Victorian times	Information / explanation	Vocabulary: dictionary and contextual work Spelling: 'cial' endings	Sentence beginnings	Writing to inform	16
Unit 2 The long and winding road ...					
1 The Jason voyage	For and against	Vocabulary: dictionary and contextual work Spelling: 'ant' words	Adjectives from nouns	For and against	22
2 Travelling tips	Advice and guidance	Vocabulary: dictionary and contextual work Spelling: 'ss' words	Active and passive voice	Advice and guidance	28
3 Farley Palace	Tourist information	Vocabulary: dictionary and contextual work Spelling: 'y' saying 'ee'	Active and passive voice	Inform and persuade	34
Unit 3 Reality and illusion					
1 Gordon the magician	Advertising	Vocabulary: dictionary and contextual work Spelling: 'cian' words	Phrasal verbs	Advertisements	40
2 Animal camouflage	Information / explanation	Vocabulary: dictionary and contextual work Spelling: 'ist' endings	Sentence beginnings	Writing to inform and explain	46
3 X-ray vision	Instructions	Vocabulary: dictionary and contextual work Spelling: 'se' words	Imperative verbs	Instructions	52

Section	Text type	Word	Sentence	Writing	Page
Unit 4 We are the champions					
1 *England win the World Cup*	Informative / entertaining article	Vocabulary: dictionary and contextual work Spelling: 'tch' words	Adverbial clauses	Writing to inform and entertain	58
2 *Taylor-made passport to the world*	Newspaper article	Vocabulary: dictionary and contextual work Spelling: words ending in 'ory'	Complex sentences	Newspaper articles	64
3 *Seize the day!*	Autobiography	Vocabulary: dictionary and contextual work Spelling: words ending in 'ise'/'yse'	Semi-colons	Autobiography	70
Unit 5 Rebel with a cause					
1 *The origin of Cool*	Biography / opinion	Vocabulary: dictionary and contextual work Spelling: double 'n' words	Pronouns	For and against	76
2 *Forms of protest*	Information	Vocabulary: dictionary and contextual work Spelling: 'eous' words	Some common mistakes	Research / information writing	82
3 *There's Something About A Convent Girl*	Autobio-graphical recount	Vocabulary: dictionary and contextual work Spelling: double 'm' words	Apostrophes	Biographical snapshots	88
Unit 6 What if ...?					
1 *All men are equal ...*	Informative / opinion	Vocabulary: dictionary and contextual work Spelling: 'ive' words	Presentational devices	Fact and opinion	94
2 *Area 51 – not of this earth*	Inform / explore	Vocabulary: dictionary and contextual work Spelling: words ending in 'ious'	Punctuation	Balanced argument	100
3 *Found: Key to Jurassic life*	Newspaper article	Vocabulary: dictionary and contextual work Spelling: words ending in 'ism'	Quotation marks	Informing and explaining	106

Unit 1 Absolute power corrupts absolutely / non-fiction

A HERO WILL RISE

GLADIATOR 15

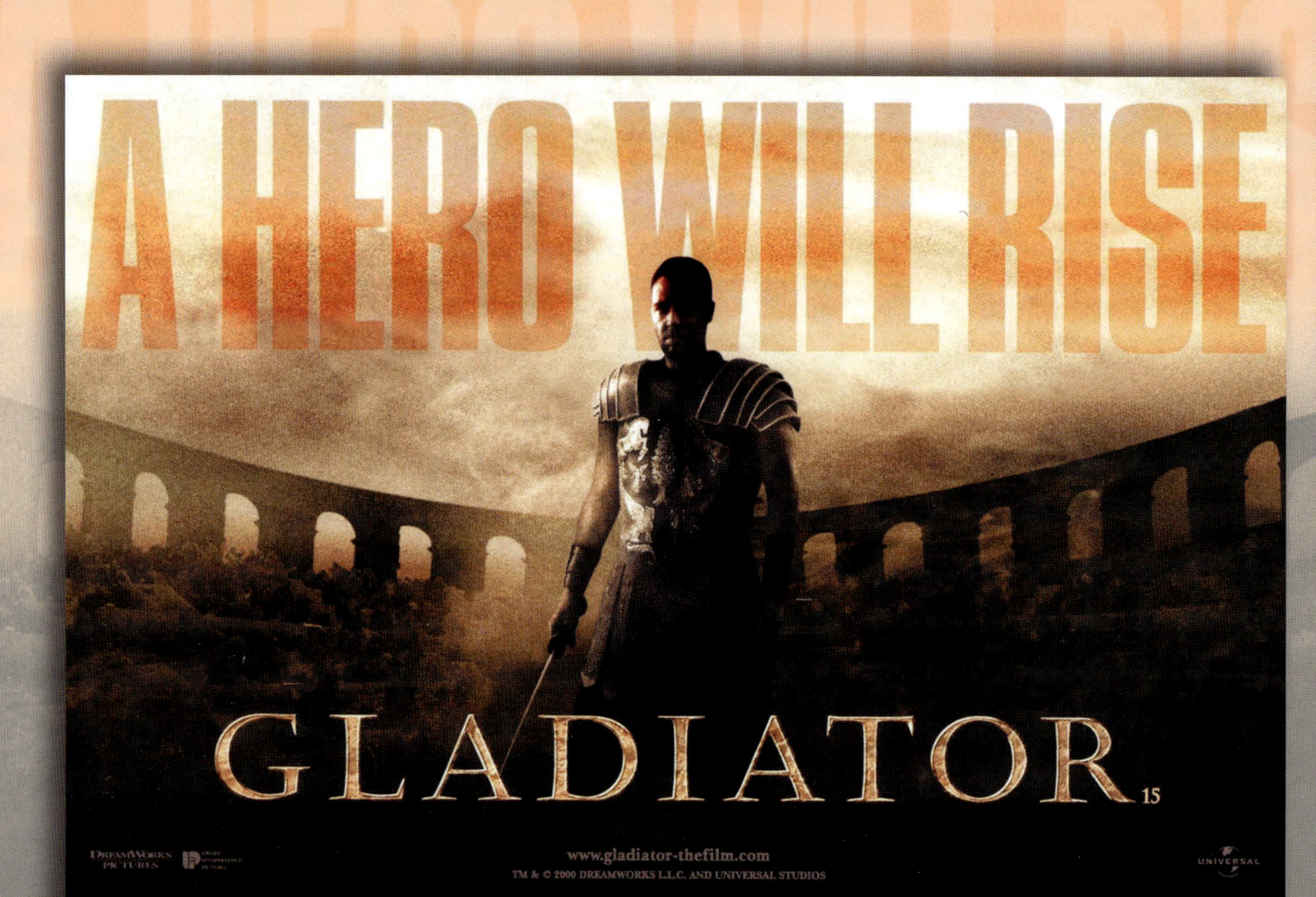

www.gladiator-thefilm.com
TM & © 2000 DREAMWORKS L.L.C. AND UNIVERSAL STUDIOS

AT CINEMAS FROM FRIDAY 12TH MAY   CHECK LOCAL PRESS FOR DETAILS

Gladiator

Release date:	2000
Running time:	2 hours 3 minutes
Cast:	Russell Crowe, Joaquin Phoenix, Richard Harris, Djimon Hounsou, Connie Nielson, Oliver Reed, Toma Arana, Derek Jacobi, Spencer Treat Clark
Director:	Ridley Scott
Producers:	David H Franzoni, Steven Spielberg, Douglas Wick
Cinematography:	John Mathieson
Music:	Hans Zimmer

Gladiator – the movie

Extract / **1.1**

Background

The time is AD 180 when the Roman Empire is at its height. Caesar Marcus Aurelius (Richard Harris) is fighting the barbarians in Germanica. He is relying on his best general, Maximus (Russell Crowe) to win him a great victory. Maximus wins the day and Caesar decides to make him his successor. Caesar's son Commodus (Joaquin Phoenix) is bitter and angry, and in his rage he kills his father. He orders Maximus to be executed. Maximus escapes and rushes home to protect his wife and child. But he is too late as Commodus has had them killed. Maximus is then captured by slave traders. He is bought from them by Proximo (Oliver Reed) who is an owner and trainer of gladiators. Very soon, Maximus finds himself fighting in the Coliseum in Rome for the entertainment of Commodus who has proclaimed himself Emperor.

Review

This is an ambitious film which has violence, treachery and romance woven into a cracking plot. The audience is gripped from the very first frame. The villains are smart and ruthless; the hero is brave and determined. The director, Ridley Scott, has created the sprawling set of Ancient Rome by attention to detail and digital technology and made it totally believable.

Russell Crowe is magnificent in the role of the gladiator. The audience understands that he is a man with nothing to lose who is driven by his determination to avenge the murder of his wife and son. Joaquin Phoenix plays the part of the evil, deranged son Commodus to perfection. While Maximus is driven by revenge, Commodus is driven by the need for absolute power. The story is gripping as we see a slave taking on the power of the Roman Emperor and we watch eagerly to see who will win.

Awards for the movie 'Gladiator'

Golden Globe:	Best Motion Picture – Drama 2001
	Best Original Score – 2001
BAFTA:	Best film – 2001
Oscars:	Best picture – 2001
	Best actor in a leading role – 2001
	Best visual effects – 2001 Best sound – 2001

COMPREHENSION

A Copy these sentences. Fill in the missing words.

1 _ _ _ _ _ _ _ _ _ _ _ directed the film *Gladiator*.
2 Steven Spielberg was one of the _ _ _ _ _ _ _ _ _ of the film.
3 At the beginning of the film, Maximus is a _ _ _ _ _ _ _ .
4 Proximo owns and trains _ _ _ _ _ _ _ _ _ _ .
5 Maximus fights before the Emperor in the _ _ _ _ _ _ _ _ .

Unit 1 Absolute power corrupts absolutely / non-fiction

B 1 Explain the following in your own words:
   a 'at its height'
   b 'wins the day'
   c 'make him his successor'.

2 Why do you think Commodus ordered the execution of Maximus?

3 What is the reviewer's opinion of Russell Crowe?

4 Why do you think the reviewer includes:
   - the information box at the beginning of the article
   - the 'awards' box at the end of the article?

C 1 In your own words, explain what the reviewer thinks of the film *Gladiator*. Quote from the review to support your answer.

2 Would this review make you go and see the film? Why? Why not?

VOCABULARY

Use a dictionary and the context of the passage to explain the meaning of the following words. They are underlined in the passage. The first one is done for you.

1	cinematography = art of making films	2	barbarians
3	proclaimed	4	ambitious
5	ruthless	6	deranged

SPELLING

'aw' words

Key word: spr**aw**ling

1 Use the key word above in a sentence of your own.

2 Learn these important **'aw'** words:

- **aw**ful
- **aw**kward
- dr**aw**
- s**aw**
- th**aw**
- withdr**aw**

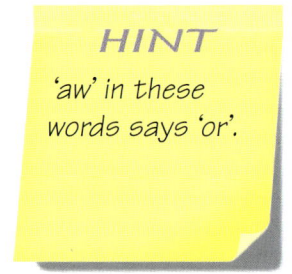

HINT
'aw' in these words says 'or'.

Gladiator – the movie

Activity / **1.1**

GRAMMAR AND PUNCTUATION

Noun and verb agreement

Remember!
Singular means one.
Plural means more than one.
Nouns and **verbs** can be singular or plural.

We use a singular noun with a singular verb,
 eg *Maximus wins* the day.
    singular noun   singular verb

We use a plural noun with a plural verb,
 eg The *barbarians fight* the Romans.
    plural noun   plural verb

HINT
It seems odd but plural nouns have *s/es* endings and singular verbs have *s/es* endings.

A Complete each sentence with the correct verb from the brackets. The first one is done for you.

1 David H Franzoni and Steven Spielberg (is / are) the film producers.
  David H Franzoni and Steven Spielberg <u>are</u> the film producers.
2 Ridley Scott (direct / directs) many films.
3 Caesar (want / wants) to make Maximus his successor.
4 The gladiators (fight / fights) to entertain the Emperor.
5 We (watch / watches) to see who will win.

HINT
Remember 'is' and 'was' are singular and 'are' and 'were' are plural.

Collective nouns are always followed by a **singular** verb,
 eg The *audience is gripped* from the very first frame.
    collective noun   singular verb

B Write whether each of these nouns would be followed by a singular verb (S) or a plural verb (P).

1 the story
2 the cast
3 the generals
4 the slave
5 the pack
6 the owner
7 the family
8 the power
9 the music
10 the film

C Choose five of the nouns from **B** and use them in sentences of your own.

Unit 1 Absolute power corrupts absolutely / non-fiction

Gladiator – the movie

Activity / **1.1**

WRITING

Information and opinion

> *Gladiator – the movie* is a film review written to:
> - **inform** the reader
> - express a personal **opinion**.

Language features

Factual information

People who are enthusiastic about films often want to know the names of the actors, directors and producers. This factual information can:
- appear in the form of a chart at the beginning of the review
- can be mentioned throughout the review.

Film enthusiasts will also be keen to know if the film has won any awards.

Background information

A reviewer will often give you an idea of the plot of a film but is careful never to give away the ending.

Opinion

Film reviewers can be very powerful. If a reviewer really dislikes a film, many people will not go to see it. If, however, a reviewer praises a film, many people feel they just have to see it.

The reviewer of *Gladiator* thinks the film is a success,
eg 'The audience is gripped ...'   '... totally believable'

Powerful vocabulary

The reviewer of *Gladiator* doesn't just say: *This is a good film. You should go and see it.* She chooses powerful vocabulary to persuade readers of how good it is,
eg 'ambitious film'   'magnificent'   'to perfection'

Writing assignment

Choose two films you have seen recently – one you liked and one you disliked. Write two short reviews so that your readers know how good you thought one of the films was and how bad the other one was.

Include:
- factual information about the actors, director, producer, etc
- background information so the reader knows some of the plot but not the ending
- your opinion as a reviewer.

Use powerful vocabulary to persuade your readers that:
- they *must* see the film
- they would be *wasting their time* if they went to see it.

Unit 1 Absolute power corrupts absolutely / non-fiction

Make the punishment fit the crime...

So you have to go to school? Blame the <u>Vile</u> Victorians! In 1870 the Education Bill was passed. The aim was ... to bring education within the reach of every English home, aye, and within the reach of those children who have no homes.

Children of the 1990s still suffer the horror of homework, the terror of teachers and the dread of school dinners. But, if you think school is bad in the twentieth century, you should have gone to school in the nineteenth!

Make the punishment fit the crime

Extract / **1.2**

Crime: Throwing ink pellets in class
Punishment:
One punishment was to kneel on the hard, rough floorboards, with your back upright and your hands placed on the back of your neck for a long period of about twenty minutes. Should you flop over, aching all over, the teacher would slap you across the head with his hand and shout <u>sternly</u>, 'Get upright, will you?'
Victorian boy

Crime: Missing Sunday church
Punishment:
Every Monday morning the priest came to each class and asked us who had missed church the day before. I always had to miss Sunday because Sunday was washing day and we only had one lot of clothes. So, week by week we admitted our <u>absence</u> and were given the strap for it. We should have been able to explain but we were ashamed to give the real reason. Once, just once, I answered back.
  'Don't you know,' the priest said, 'that God loves you and wants to see you in His house on Sundays?'
  'But if he loves us, why does he want us to get the strap on Monday?' I asked.
I don't remember what the priest said, but I do know I got a double load of stripes when he'd gone.
Victorian girl

Crime: Being late for school
Punishment:
With no exams at the end of your school life, the chance of a good job after school depended on your final report – your reference. One boy was kept back by his father and so was late for school ... The only boy in the school to be late. I was <u>humiliated</u> in front of three hundred boys by the headmaster and afterwards got six mighty slashes on the fingers with a thin cane. My God, it hurt, believe me. And something else which hurt even more. My name was <u>inserted</u> in the <u>disgrace</u> and punishment book and put on record for future reference.
Victorian boy

From *The Vile Victorians* by Terry Deary

COMPREHENSION

A Write 'true' or 'false' for each of these statements.

1 The punishment for throwing ink pellets was the cane.
2 The Victorian girl always missed church on Sunday.
3 The punishment for missing church was the strap.
4 The chance of a good job depended on your final school report.
5 If you were late for school you had to kneel on the floor.

Unit 1 Absolute power corrupts absolutely / non-fiction

B 1 Explain the following in your own words:
  a 'within the reach of'
  b 'was kept back'
  c 'for future reference'.

2 What does the Victorian girl mean when she says 'we were ashamed to give the real reason'?

3 Why do you think she 'got a double load of stripes' when the priest had gone?

4 In what way did having his name in the punishment book 'hurt even more' than the slashes with the cane?

C Look at each of the personal recounts about life in a Victorian school. For each one find and quote:
- an example of something that happened
- an example of how the writer felt about it.

VOCABULARY

Use a dictionary and the context of the passage to explain the meaning of the following words. They are underlined in the passage. The first one is done for you.

1 vile = hateful
2 sternly
3 absence
4 humiliated
5 inserted
6 disgrace

SPELLING

Compound words

Key word: head + master = **headmaster**

1 Use the key word above in a sentence of your own.

2 Learn these important '**compound**' words:

crosshatch   meanwhile

flowchart   multimedia

highlight   spreadsheet

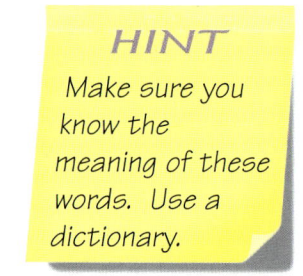

HINT
Make sure you know the meaning of these words. Use a dictionary.

Make the punishment fit the crime Activity / 1.2

GRAMMAR AND PUNCTUATION

Alliteration

> **Alliteration** is where words next to each other, or near each other, in a sentence begin with the same sound,
>
> eg *'horror of homework'*
>   *'terror of teachers'*
>
> Alliteration is used to call attention to certain words.

A Copy these sentences. Underline the alliterative sounds. The first one is done for you.

1 The fair breeze blew, the white foam flew.

   The fair breeze blew, the white foam flew.

2 The green grass grew strong.

3 She sells sea shells on the sea shore.

4 Rain rattled on the rear windows.

5 My mother made marmalade.

B Put an adjective in front of each of these nouns to make an alliterative phrase. The first one is done for you.

1 sea   *savage sea*   2 dagger
3 beach   4 tree
5 lion   6 cave

C Make your alliterative phrases into sentences by adding a verb beginning with the same sound. The first one is done for you.

The savage sea swirled around the cliffs.

> **HINT**
> Add any other words you need.

D Write your name down the left side of your page. Make alliterative sentences from the **sound** of each letter in your name. The sentences can be as silly as you like. Here is how it is done.

E Eight enormous earthquakes erupted everywhere.

T Toasted teacakes taste terrible.

H Happy hippos hardly hop.

A Angry ants annoy antelopes.

N Noisy knights noticed nothing.

What do you notice about the sentence for N?

> **HINT**
> If your first name just happens to be Ethan, use your surname.

Unit 1 Absolute power corrupts absolutely / non-fiction

Make the punishment fit the crime

Activity / **1.2**

WRITING

Recounts / autobiography

> Writing a **recount** of something that has happened to you is like writing a small biography. The recounts in the passage:
> - tell the reader what happened – the facts
> - let the reader see how the writer felt about what happened.

Language features

Writing in the first person

The writers avoided beginning every sentence with 'I' or 'we' by:
- using time phrases: *'Every Monday morning ...'*
- reordering words in a sentence:
  'So, week by week we admitted our absence'

NOT   *We admitted our absence week by week.*

Facts

The reader needs to know very clearly what has happened – the facts,
  eg *'the teacher would slap you across the head with his hand ...'*
      'Every Monday morning the priest came to each class ...'

Feelings

Personal recounts are not just a list of 'what happened when'. The writer says how he / she feels about what has happened,
  eg *'aching all over'*   *'My God, it hurt, believe me.'*

Adjectives and adverbs

The writer uses powerful adjectives and adverbs,
  eg *'shout sternly'*   *'mighty slashes'*

Past tense

A recount is a piece of writing about something that happened in the past, so the writer uses the past tense,
  eg *'we admitted our absence'*   *'My name was inserted ...'*

Writing assignment

Write a personal recount of a time when you where punished either at home or at school. Let the reader know what happened and how you felt about it. Remember to use suitable adjectives and adverbs, and to write in the past tense.

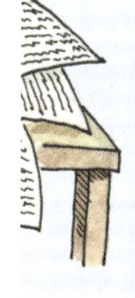

Unit 1 Absolute power corrupts absolutely / non-fiction

I thee wed …

Marriage in Victorian times

Most people today marry because they fall in love. In the nineteenth century, there were often other reasons for marrying, the main one being <u>financial</u>. Power and money formed the basis of many marriages in the upper classes. Marrying someone who was upper-class was important if you were upper-class. The upper classes liked to keep money and property to themselves!

The eldest son

The eldest son was expected to run the estate after his father's death. If he could increase the wealth and power of the family, so much the better.

Marriage in Victorian times

Extract / **1.3**

It was most important that the eldest son in an upper-class family married 'well'. There were several reasons for this:
- He would <u>inherit</u> his father's 'estate' – that is, any money and property the family had.
- If his father had a title, he would also inherit that.
- If the family had money but no property, the eldest son needed to marry into a family with property so that they could become even richer.
- If the family had property but no 'ready cash', he needed to marry into a family with plenty of money.

The other children
It was also important that the other children in the family married well. When two people got married there would be a marriage 'settlement'. Both the bride and groom would be given money or property, or both, by the parents. This would take wealth out of the family and leave less for the eldest son to inherit. Many families got around this by marrying their children to close relatives, eg cousins, so they kept the money 'in the family'.

Younger sons were not so <u>fortunate</u> as the firstborn son. As the upper classes did not like to split up their estates, they received very little. <u>Consequently</u>, they were encouraged to find an heiress as a wife. They did, however, have more freedom to choose a career. Going into the military, the church or even politics was encouraged as they did not have to run the family estate.

Conclusion
Marriage for the upper classes in the nineteenth century was designed to keep power and wealth in the hands of those who already had it. This would not happen if a poor person married into a rich family, bringing no money, property or power with them. It was seen as the duty of the eldest son to marry well and have <u>heirs</u> so that the estate did not fall into anyone else's hands. Their job was to carry on the family name and increase the family wealth.

Bibliography J V Beckett, *The <u>Aristocracy</u> in England 1640–1914* (New York, 1986).
John Habakkuk, *Marriage, Debt and the Estates System* (Oxford, 1994).

COMPREHENSION

A Choose the best answer for each statement.

1. Upper classes in the nineteenth century usually married:
   a for love
   b for money
   c for a career.

2. The eldest son was expected to:
   a become a soldier
   b stay unmarried
   c run the family estate.

3. Younger children often married:
   a close relatives
   b poor people
   c politicians.

4. Younger children inherited:
   a the same as the eldest son
   b more than the eldest son
   c less than the eldest son.

5. Eldest sons had to:
   a marry an heiress
   b carry on the family name
   c go into the church.

Unit 1 Absolute power corrupts absolutely / non-fiction

B 1 Explain the following in your own words:
  a *'so much the better'*
  b *'a title'*
  c *'got around this'*.

2 In what way was a younger son:
  - less fortunate than the eldest son
  - more fortunate than the eldest son?

3 What do you think would happen if an eldest son wanted to marry a poor woman?

4 Explain in your own words why nineteenth-century upper-class families married into other upper-class families.

C Explain why the writer has used:
  - bullet points
  - subheadings.

VOCABULARY

Use a dictionary and the context of the passage to explain the meaning of the following words. They are underlined in the passage. The first one is done for you.

1 financial = *to do with money*
2 inherit
3 fortunate
4 consequently
5 heirs
6 aristocracy

SPELLING

'cial' endings

Key word: finan**cial**

1 Use the key word above in a sentence of your own.

2 Learn these important **'cial'** words:

- benefi**cial**
- ra**cial**
- commer**cial**
- so**cial**
- espe**cial**ly
- spe**cial**

> **HINT**
> Make sure you know the meaning of these words. Use a dictionary.

Marriage in Victorian times

Activity / **1.3**

GRAMMAR AND PUNCTUATION

Sentence beginnings

> **Beginning sentences** in different ways makes writing more interesting.
>
> When we write, we usually think of the subject of a sentence first and use the subject to begin the sentence,
>
> > eg *The eldest son would also inherit a title, if his father had one.*
>
> The writer of 'I thee wed' has used different ways to avoid beginning every sentence with the subject.
>
> - 'if' clauses, eg *'If his father had a title, he would also inherit that.'*
> - 'ing' clauses, eg *'Marrying someone who was upper-class was important if you were upper-class.'*

A Rewrite these sentences so that the 'if' clause comes at the beginning. The first one is done for you.

1. The eldest son needed to marry someone with money if the family had no ready cash.

   If the family had no ready cash, the eldest son needed to marry someone with money.

2. The other children had to marry well if the family's wealth was to be safe.
3. Younger sons should marry an heiress if they could find one.
4. Younger sons could go into the military, church or politics if they wanted a career.
5. The eldest son would have to run the estate if the father died.

B Rewrite these sentences so that they begin with an 'ing' clause. The first one is done for you.

1. It was possible that the younger son could have a career.

   Having a career was a possibility for the younger son.

2. It was thought to be a good idea to marry a close relative.
3. It was seen as a duty of the eldest son to marry well.
4. It was less important to marry for love than for money.
5. The eldest son was expected to carry on the family name.

> **HINT**
> You will have to make some changes in each sentence so that it makes sense.

Unit 1 Absolute power corrupts absolutely / non-fiction

Marriage in Victorian times

Activity / **1.3**

WRITING

Writing to inform

> The purpose of the article 'Marriage in Victorian times' is to inform readers of the attitude to marriage in the nineteenth century.

Language features

Main heading

If the purpose of a piece of writing is to inform the reader, it must be clear from the very beginning what that piece of writing is about. The main heading does this job:

Marriage in Victorian times

Subheadings

Subheadings are used to 'break up' the information into sections. Each section deals with one aspect of the topic.

- The paragraph after the main heading introduces the topic. This can have the subheading 'Introduction' but it is not really necessary.
- The subheading '**The eldest son**' lets the reader concentrate on what the eldest son had to think about before getting married.
- The subheading '**The other children**' alerts the reader to the fact that the situation was different for these children.
- The subheading '**Conclusion**' summarises how marriage was conducted in the nineteenth century.

The facts

To write a piece of information text, the writer has to know the facts,

eg *'Power and money formed the basis of many marriages in the upper classes.'*

Bibliography

This is a list of books the writer used to research the facts about marriage in Victorian times. These are a writer's 'sources'.

Writing assignment

Research one of the following:
- the type of work poor Victorian children had to do
- a famous Victorian author, eg Charles Dickens
- Queen Victoria.

Write an article to inform readers about the topic you have chosen. Use:
- a main heading so a reader knows what the article is about
- subheadings to divide up the information.

Keep a list of sources and include a biography.

Unit 2 The long and winding road.../non-fiction

The Jason voyage...

The Jason voyage

Extract / **2.1**

Most people first come across the story of *Jason and the Argonauts* in school. I read the story in an anthology of Greek myths and it has been one of my favourites ever since. I was thrilled by the idea of a long and dangerous voyage; of a boat that could speak with a human voice; and the heroic deeds of the Argonauts. But could the voyage have actually happened?

As I got older, I did some research into the story. The voyage was said to have taken place in the thirteenth century BC. All scholars agreed *where* Jason's voyage was alleged to have started and ended. The boat, the *Argo*, set off from Greece and voyaged to the far eastern end of the Black Sea in a kingdom called Colchis, which we now know as Soviet Georgia. But as the voyage happened so long ago, surely there is no evidence left of the route the boat took?

Although the scholars agreed on where the boat went, they did not agree on anything else. Some said that the story of Jason and the Argonauts was just that – a story. Others said that they believed there was a grain of truth in the story but, over time, it had been wildly exaggerated. They support their view by saying that the first full-length account of the story was not written down until a thousand years after it was supposed to have happened!

Some scholars believe that the voyage would have been impossible. A Bronze Age boat could not have made the 1500-mile journey. The strength of the currents in the Bosphorus would have been far too strong for such a primitive boat. It would have been wrecked or fallen to pieces. The type of boat which could have made the journey needed to be one with fifty oars on two levels, one above the other. Maritime historians tell us that a boat of this type and power did not exist before the end of the eighth century BC.

So, we are left with two important questions. Is the account of Jason's voyage just a made-up story, or did a much shorter voyage take place which has been exaggerated over time?

COMPREHENSION

A Copy these sentences. Fill in the missing words.

1. The author first read about the Jason story at _ _ _ _ _ _.
2. The *Argo* was an unusual boat because it could _ _ _ _ _.
3. Most scholars agree where the voyage began and _ _ _ _ _.
4. It would have taken a boat of _ _ _ _ _ oars to make such a journey.
5. The boat that could have made such a voyage was not built until the end of the _ _ _ _ _ _ century BC.

Unit 2 The long and winding road ... / non-fiction

B 1 Explain the following in your own words:
   a *'heroic deeds'*
   b *'grain of truth'*
   c *'wildly exaggerated'*.

2 What is it about the voyage that all scholars agree on?

3 Why is it unlikely that any new evidence can be found?

4 For what reason do some scholars think that the voyage could not have taken place in the thirteenth century BC?

C Do you think the voyage really happened or is it just a story?
Give reasons for your answer.

VOCABULARY

Use a dictionary and the context of the extract to explain the meaning of the following words. They are underlined in the passage. The first one is done for you.

1 anthology = *collection*   2 alleged

3 evidence   4 scholars

5 primitive   6 maritime

SPELLING

'ant' words

Key word: import**ant**

1 Use the key word above in a sentence of your own.

2 Learn these important **'ant'** words:

conson**ant**	immigr**ant**
depend**ant**	Protest**ant**
dist**ant**	relev**ant**

HINT

Make sure you know the meaning of each word. Use a dictionary.

24

The Jason voyage

Activity / 2.1

GRAMMAR AND PUNCTUATION

Adjectives from nouns

> **Adjectives** make writing more interesting. They help the reader 'see' what you are writing about.
>
> Some adjectives can be formed from nouns,
>   eg noun = hero   adjective = hero**ic**

A Make adjectives from these nouns. They all end in 'ic'.
The first one is done for you.

1 asthma   *asthmatic*
2 poet
3 microscope
4 system
5 magnet
6 volcano

HINT
Use a dictionary to check your spelling.

B Use two of the 'ic' adjectives you have formed in **A** in sentences of your own.

C Make adjectives from these nouns. They all end in 'ous'.
The first one is done for you.

1 courtesy   *courteous*
2 danger
3 glory
4 fame
5 nerve
6 disaster

D Use two of the 'ous' adjectives you have formed in **C** in sentences of your own.

E Make adjectives from these nouns. They all end in 'ful'.
The first one is done for you.

1 care   *careful*
2 fear
3 hope
4 skill
5 truth
6 doubt

F Use two of the 'ful' adjectives you have formed in **E** in sentences of your own.

G Make adjectives from these nouns. They all end in 'ish'.
The first one is done for you.

1 fiend   *fiendish*
2 style
3 book
4 fever
5 brute
6 child

H Use two of the 'ish' adjectives you have formed in **G** in sentences of your own.

Unit 2 The long and winding road ... / non-fiction

The Jason voyage

Activity / 2.1

WRITING

For and against

One type of non-fiction writing:
- introduces a topic, eg The Voyage of the Argonauts
- puts forward arguments **for** it being true
- puts forward arguments **against** it being true.

Language features

First person

The article is written in the first person. The author is presenting the arguments he has researched,
   eg 'I read the story ...'   'As I got older ...'

First paragraph

The author uses the first paragraph to:
- give details about the story
- explain his personal 'fascination' with the voyage.

Facts

The writer includes 'facts' in the sense of what is 'thought' might have happened,
   eg 'the voyage **was said to** have taken place ...'
       'Jason's voyage was **alleged** to have started ...'

Arguments for and against

The writer looks at different views:
   'Some said that the story of Jason and the Argonauts was just that – a story.'
   'Others said that they believed there was a grain of truth in the story'

Writing assignment

Did the Americans really land on the moon or did they 'fake' it?
Write an article which puts forward:
- the view that it actually happened
- the view that it was 'faked'.

You will need to:
- research the facts of the moon landing
- use these facts to support the view that it took place
- think carefully about / research how it could have been 'faked' and use these ideas to put forward the opposite point of view.

Unit 2 The long and winding road... / non-fiction

... do some travelling ...

Travelling tips

Extract / 2.2

Travelling tips

If you can, make sure you do some travelling before you become an adult and you have lots of <u>responsibilities</u> to worry about. Do something special and see a little of the rest of the world. Here are some tips which are worth reading before you set off.

- Where possible, leave a copy of your route with your family and inform them of any changes in your plans. **Never hitch-hike.**
- If you are travelling on your own, don't drink alcohol if you need to be alert.
- Phone home at least every couple of weeks.
- Book accommodation in advance if you plan to arrive in a town late at night.
- Try to observe and respect local customs, particularly about the way people dress.
- If you can't bear to lose something, don't take it with you in the first place.
- Always get good travel insurance.
- Don't count your money in public.
- Take some spare passport photos. Also take a photocopy of your passport (front cover, page with the number and personal details) and any <u>valid</u> visas in your passport. Keep these in a separate place to your passport.
- **Never** take anyone else's luggage through customs or leave your bags unattended at airports.
- Don't worry too much about whether your trip will work out, just do it!

If things go wrong …

Things can get difficult if you are abroad and your money, your tickets or your passport are lost or stolen, so take <u>precautions</u> before you go – it's worth the effort.

- Make a note of the serial numbers of your traveller's cheques, if you have them.
- Find out the telephone numbers of the British Embassies in the countries you will be visiting.
- Carry traveller's cheques and cash separately.
- Never give your passport to anyone, including car hire agencies.

If you do have problems whilst abroad, the Embassy can:

- Give you an emergency passport, and contact your family / friends so they can help out with money or tickets.
- Help you with local <u>procedures</u>, if you've been in an accident, for example.
- Put you in touch with <u>interpreters</u>, lawyers and doctors.
- Sometimes cash a cheque for up to £50, if you have a banker's card.

However, the Embassy cannot:

- Pay your debts or medical costs.
- Influence the local authorities if you are charged with an <u>offence</u>.

Travelling abroad

COMPREHENSION

A Write 'true' or 'false' for each of these statements.

1 Don't tell anyone where you are going.
2 Make sure you have good travel insurance.
3 Carry cash and traveller's cheques together.
4 The Embassy can give you an emergency passport.
5 The Embassy can pay your debts.

Unit 2 The long and winding road... / non-fiction

B 1 Explain the following in your own words:
   a 'need to be alert'
   b 'in advance'
   c 'can't bear to'.

2 Why do you think you are advised to 'phone home at least every couple of weeks'?

3 Why do you think you are advised not to 'count your money in public'?

4 Why do you think you should 'never give your passport to anyone'?

C Explain the reasons why you think the guidance has been set out in this way. Why has the writer used:
- subheadings
- bullet points
- bold text.

VOCABULARY

Use a dictionary and the context of the extract to explain the meaning of the following words. They are underlined in the passage. The first one is done for you.

1 responsibilities = *obligations*   2 valid

3 precautions   4 procedures

5 interpreters   6 offence

SPELLING

'ss' words

Key words: po**ss**ible   dre**ss**   pa**ss**port

1 Use these key words above in sentences of your own.

2 Learn these important '**ss**' words:

embarra**ss**   gue**ss**

expre**ss**ion   nece**ss**ary

discu**ss**ion   succe**ss**

HINT
Make sure you know the meaning of each word. Use a dictionary.

30

Travelling tips

Activity / **2.2**

GRAMMAR AND PUNCTUATION

Active and passive voice

> **Remember:** in a sentence:
> - the subject does the action
> - the verb is the action
> - the object has the action done to it.
>
>   The thief stole the passport.
>   subject active verb object
>
> This pattern: subject + active verb + object = **active voice**
>
> Some sentences have a different pattern.
> The passport was stolen by the thief.
>   object   passive verb   subject
>
> This pattern: object + passive verb + subject = **passive voice**

A Change these sentences from active to passive voice. The first one is done for you.

1 Most people enjoy holidays.
   Holidays are enjoyed by most people.

2 Tourists can ruin exotic places.

3 Tour operators can overcharge tourists.

4 Tourists should take care of their possessions.

5 Tourists can get help from their Embassy.

B Change these sentences from passive to active voice. The first one is done for you.

1 A passport is needed by everyone travelling abroad.
   Everyone travelling abroad will need a passport.

2 Cash and traveller's cheques should be carried separately.

3 Tickets should be checked by travellers before they leave.

4 Money should not be counted in public.

5 Your debts cannot be paid by the Embassy.

HINT

Sometimes you have to add the subject 'you'.

Unit 2 The long and winding road ... / non-fiction

Travelling tips

Activity / **2.2**

WRITING

Advice and guidance

> In some situations it is useful to get **advice and guidance** from someone who knows what they are talking about.
> They can tell you:
> - what to expect
> - how to avoid problems
> - how to get the best out of a situation / experience / machine, etc.
>
> *Travelling abroad* is a web article giving tips and guidance to help the reader have a pleasant, hassle-free experience when travelling.

Language features

Style and structure

To help the reader, the writer has used:
- subheadings, eg *'If things go wrong ...'*
- bullet points, eg • *'Don't count your money in public.'*

Imperative verbs

Imperative verbs are used in writing which instructs, advises or guides,

eg *'**Try** to observe ...'* ie You should try to observe ...

*'**Phone** home ...'* ie You should phone home ...

By using imperative verbs you avoid needless repetition and get straight to the point.

Personal / direct style

The writer speaks to each individual reader by the use of the second person,

eg *'If **you** are travelling on your own ...'*

*'Never give **your** passport to anyone ...'*

Writing assignment

Write guidance and advice for someone wanting to take a long-distance journey by one of the following methods:
- train
- car
- aeroplane.

Think of:
- what they should do / get before they go
- what they should do to be safe and comfortable on their journey.

Use:
- subheadings
- bullet points
- imperative verbs.

Unit 2 The long and winding road ... / non-fiction

A popular attraction ...

Farley Palace

The Duke and Duchess of Farley welcome you to their home. Tour the house; enjoy the lovely gardens; and attend the special events throughout the year.

The first Duke of Farley was a successful soldier in many battles against Louis XIV of France. He was handsomely rewarded and a magnificent house was built with the money he received. The Palace was designed by Sir Christopher Wren.

Stone was transported from as many as thirty quarries and the finished building, with courtyards, covers five acres.

The finest artists of the day were employed to paint the ceilings with scenes of the Duke's famous victories.

The Great Hall is 20 metres in height and lavishly furnished with tapestries, sculptures and paintings.

The Palace is still owned by the Farleys and the 9th Duke and his family reside there to this day.

Farley Palace

Extract / 2.3

OPENING TIMES
The Palace and Gardens are open from March to October from 10am to 5pm.

ADMISSION
Adults: £10.00
Children under 15 and OAPs: £5.00

Details of season tickets can be obtained from the Tourist Information Centre.

THE PALACE
Guided tours of the Palace take place every half hour.

THE GARDENS
To the east of the Palace is the Rose Garden.

To the west of the Palace are formal gardens with delightful walks around spectacular fountains.

The extensive maze, overlooked by the Great Hall, is a popular attraction for children.

ADDITIONAL INFORMATION

WHERE TO EAT
- The *Farley Café*: self-service restaurant serving sandwiches, cakes and pastries.
- The *Duke's Restaurant*: waitress service of two- and three-course lunches and cream teas.

WHERE TO SHOP
- The *Stable Shop*: this can be found next to the main entrance and has a wide selection of superb gifts and mementoes.
- The *Book Shop*: next to the Duke's Restaurant, the shop has a wide range of books on the history of the Palace from the 18th century to the present day.

SPECIAL EVENTS
Each year the Palace hosts special events such as classical and pop concerts; art exhibitions; dog shows and fêtes. For forthcoming events, pick up the Diary of Events from the Tourist Information Centre.

COMPREHENSION

A Choose the best answer for each statement.

1. The first Duke of Farley was:
   a an artist   **b** a soldier   **c** a builder.

2. The Palace was built of:
   a brick   **b** wood   **c** stone.

3. The Tourist Information Centre has information about:
   a special events   **b** where to eat   **c** where to shop.

4. The Stable Shop sells:
   a books   **b** gifts   **c** food.

5. The present owner of Farley Palace is:
   a Christopher Wren   **b** the first Duke   **c** the 9th Duke.

Unit 2   The long and winding road ... / non-fiction

B 1 Explain the following in your own words:
   a *'handsomely rewarded'*
   b *'finest artists of the day'*
   c *'forthcoming events'*.

   2 Who do you think rewarded the Duke of Farley for his success in battle?

   3 What was Sir Christopher Wren's profession?

   4 What do you understand by the term *'season ticket'*?

C If you were planning to visit Farley Palace, would the information in the brochure be useful? Think about:
   - how the information is set out
   - any other information (text / pictures / diagrams) which would make the brochure more useful.

VOCABULARY

Use a dictionary and the context of the extract to explain the meaning of the following words. They are underlined in the brochure. The first one is done for you.

1 transported = *carried*   **2** lavishly

3 reside   **4** extensive

5 superb   **6** mementoes

SPELLING

'y' saying 'ee'

Key word: centur**y**

   1 Use the key word above in a sentence of your own. Remember: when nouns end in a consonant and 'y', they usually make their plurals by changing the 'y' to 'i and adding 'es', eg activit**y** activit**ies**.

   2 Learn these important **'y' saying 'ee'** words.

   abilit**y**   injur**y**

   activit**y**   povert**y**

   authorit**y**   safet**y**

36

Farley Palace

Activity / 2.3

GRAMMAR AND PUNCTUATION

Active and passive voice

> **Remember!** In a sentence:
> - the subject does the action
> - the verb is the action
> - the object has the action done to it.
>
> *The Duke won the battle.*
> subject   verb   object
>
> This pattern: subject + active verb + object = **active voice**

A Copy these active sentences. Underline:
  - the subject in red
  - the verb in blue
  - the object in green.

The first one is done for you.

1 Sir Christopher Wren designed Farley Palace.
  Sir Christopher Wren designed Farley Palace.
2 Artists painted the ceilings.
3 The Great Hall overlooks the maze.
4 The Farley café sells sandwiches.
5 The Palace hosts special events.

> Some sentences have a different pattern.
> *The battle was won by the Duke.*
> object   verb   subject
>
> This pattern: object + verb + subject = **passive voice**.

B Copy these passive sentences. Underline:
  - the object in green
  - the verb in blue
  - the subject in red.

The first one is done for you.

1 A magnificent house was built by the Duke.
  A magnificent house was built by the Duke.
2 The Palace is visited by many tourists.
3 Visitors are welcomed by the Duke and Duchess.
4 Lunch is served by waitresses.
5 History books are sold by the Book Shop.

C Change the **active** sentences in **A** to **passive** sentences.

D Change the **passive** sentences in **B** to **active** sentences.

Unit 2 The long and winding road ... / non-fiction

Farley Palace

Activity / 2.3

WRITING

Inform and persuade

The brochure on Farley Palace is non-fiction writing which gives the reader **information** and uses description to **persuade** people to visit.

Language features

Information

- People visiting a tourist attraction like to know something about it. The brochure begins with some historical information,

  eg *'The Palace was designed by Sir Christopher Wren.'*

- The brochure gives the reader useful, practical pieces of information,

  eg *'The Palace and Gardens are open from March to October from 10am to 5pm.'*

Vocabulary

The vocabulary is chosen carefully to persuade people that this is an interesting place to visit,

  eg *'lavishly furnished'*   *'delightful walks'*   *'spectacular fountains'*.

Layout

The information is clearly laid out using:

- colour
- bullet points
- different fonts
- bold
- subheadings
- italics.

Writing assignment

Choose one of the following places:

- a famous football stadium
- a theme park
- a castle.

Use books and the web to find information, and keep a list of your sources.

Make notes on what you find out.

Design a brochure which informs people about the place and persuades them to visit it.

Think carefully about:

- the text
- the pictures
- the layout.

Unit 3 Reality and illusion / non-fiction

Magic Show...

Gordon the Magician Presents...
Readers, Winners & Magic!

Gordon's wild imagination has created yet another Original Magic Extravaganza. Gordon has assembled a crazy cast of characters to entertain your audience. These Crazy Characters "Go for the Gold" with hilarious comedy magic and funny situations. Kids participate! Audience members come up front and join the show, helping McFly the Rabbit and Barney the Book become "Reading Winners"!

"You will never be sure if you are just watching the show or becoming part of it!"

Be a winner. Reserve your date today.

Gordon's show is compact enough to play the smallest quiet corner yet can expand in minutes to fill a large stage. This fun packed, fast paced show is a must for your summer reading programme. Gordon brings everything he needs for his programme: Professional Sound System, Music, Magical Props and his wealth of experience entertaining young people... all you do is provide the audience.

McFly the Rabbit

I can't wait to see Gordon's show.

Barney the Book

To Book Your Show
Call Paula Kreuter at Performing Artist Management
248-879-1943
E-mail pemgnt@aol.com

Other Shows Available!
Mystery of the Lost Library Card, Fun Comedy Show, Michigan Magic Show & More!
Visit Gordon's web site www.GordontheMagician.com

Gordon the magician

Extract / **3.1**

COMPREHENSION

A Copy these sentences. Fill in the missing words.

1 Gordon's show has a crazy cast of _ _ _ _ _ _ _ _ _ _.
2 Members of the _ _ _ _ _ _ _ take part in the show.
3 Gordon has experience of entertaining _ _ _ _ _ _ _ _ _ _ _.
4 You can also go and see Mystery of the Lost _ _ _ _ _ _ _ Card.
5 Gordon's e-mail address is _ _ _ _ _ _ _ _ _ _. _ _.

41

Unit 3 Reality and illusion / non-fiction

B 1 Explain the following in your own words:
   a *'wild imagination'*
   b *'fast paced show'*
   c *'wealth of experience'*.

2 Do you think the poster is aimed at:
   - parents
   - children
   - both?

   Give your reasons.

3 How do you know that Gordon can perform his show anywhere?

4 What are the two ways you can book tickets for the show?

C How do you think the poster persuades people to go to Gordon's show? You should comment on:
   - the use of colour
   - the various presentational devices
   - the language
   - the illustrations.

VOCABULARY

Use a dictionary and the context of the passage to explain the meaning of the following words. They are underlined in the passage. The first one is done for you.

1 extravaganza = *spectacular event*
2 assembled
3 hilarious
4 participate
5 compact
6 available

SPELLING

'cian' words

Key word: magi**cian**

1 Use the key word above in a sentence of your own.

2 Learn these important **'cian'** words:

   beauti**cian**   physi**cian**

   electri**cian**   politi**cian**

   musi**cian**   techni**cian**

> **HINT**
> The ending 'cian', which sounds like 'shun', is usually used for a person who has a particular job or skill.

42

Gordon the magician

Activity / **3.1**

GRAMMAR AND PUNCTUATION

Phrasal verbs

> We often use verbs with the following words:
>
> in   on   up   away   round   about   over
> by   off   down back   through along   forward
>
> These are called **phrasal verbs**,
>   eg *think about* = ponder
>   *broke down* = stopped working

A Use the phrasal verbs in the box below to complete each sentence.
The first one is done for you.

| moving in | cross out | took off | closed down | breaking down |

1 The burglars got into the bank by _____ the door.
  The burglars got into the bank by breaking down the door.

2 _____ any mistakes you make.

3 The shop on the corner has _____.

4 When are you _____ to your new house?

5 I was excited when the plane _____.

B Write a synonym for each of the phrasal verbs below.
The first one is done for you.

1 blow up = *explode*   2 put up with
3 put out   4 do away with
5 hand in   6 stand for
7 find out   8 leave out
9 make up   10 bring about
11 look up to   12 throw up
13 put off   14 speed up
15 point out   16 pull out

> **HINT**
> A synonym is a word which means the same or nearly the same as another word or words.

C Use these phrasal verbs in sentences of your own.

1 drive off   2 fill in
3 wake up   4 throw away

43

Unit 3 Reality and illusion / non-fiction

44

Gordon the magician

Activity / **3.1**

WRITING

Advertisements

> The **advertisement** for *Gordon the Magician* is intended to persuade people to go to see the show. A good advertisement:
> - is eye-catching
> - gives information
> - uses persuasive language.

Language features

Presentational devices

Advertisers think carefully about:
- layout of the page, eg headings, subheadings, graphics, columns, captions
- fonts, eg size, typeface, colour, bold, italic
- graphics, eg photographs, cartoons, logos, colours, angles, symbols.

Information

Part of the job of an advertisement is to give information,

　　eg *'E-mail pemgnt@aol.com'*

　　　'Gordon brings everything he needs for his programme'

Persuasion

If the advertisement said: 'Gordon's show is very good' it wouldn't really persuade you to go to see it. The writer chooses powerful vocabulary to persuade you,

　　eg *'wild imagination'*　　*'hilarious comedy magic'*　　*'fast paced'*

Audience

A writer of advertisements must think carefully about who the advertisement is aimed at. For example, it would be silly to use very sophisticated language if the advertisement was aimed at 5-year-olds.

Writing assignment

Make an advertisement for a magazine to advertise one of the following:

| a concert for a popular band | a fun toothpaste for young children | a holiday for people over 60 |

Remember:
- think about your audience
- use text and illustrations
- include information people will need
- use persuasive language.

45

Unit 3   Reality and illusion / non-fiction

Now you see me, now you don't...

Animal camouflage

Squirrel

Camouflage:
the natural colouring of an animal which enables it to blend in with its surroundings.

Animals in the wild have two major problems: how to find food and how to avoid *being* food! Almost every animal has other animals which feed on it. These animals are known as predators. One way in which nature helps animals to survive is the art of camouflage. If another animal cannot see you, it cannot eat you.

Zoologists have studied animals to see how they protect themselves with camouflage.

Dolphin

Blending in
The simplest camouflage technique for an animal is to blend in with its surroundings. This need to be overlooked is often the reason why animals are the colours they are. For example, deer and squirrels are a soft brownish colour which helps them to blend in with the brown colour of trees and soil. Many sea creatures such as sharks and dolphins are a blue-grey colour to blend in with the soft, underwater light.

Changing colour
Being able to blend in with the surroundings is a useful trick but what if the surroundings change? Some animals have the ability to change what they look like depending on their changing surroundings.

Animal camouflage

Extract / **3.2**

The **Arctic fox** can change the colour of its coat. In spring and summer is has brown fur to blend in with the soil and plants. When snow falls in winter, its fur changes to white.

Chameleons are found in the forests of Madagascar. They can change from bright green to dark brown to blend in with their surroundings.

Disguise

Another way animals have of protecting themselves is the art of disguise. If they don't look like an animal but resemble something else, a predator will pass them by.

The **walking stick** is an insect which looks just like a twig. It is not that a predator doesn't see the insect. It sees it but thinks it is just a twig.

COMPREHENSION

A Write 'true' or 'false' for each of these statements.
1 A predator is an animal which feeds on other animals.
2 Squirrels cannot blend into their background.
3 Animals change their colour because they want to be seen.
4 The Arctic fox is found in Madagascar.
5 The walking stick is a twig-like insect.

47

Unit 3 Reality and illusion / non-fiction

B 1 Explain what is meant by the following expressions:
   a *'blend in with its surroundings'*
   b *'the need to be overlooked'*
   c *'pass them by'*.

2 Explain in your own words why an animal's colour is important to its survival.

3 Why do animals need to change colour?

4 Explain the difference between an animal which camouflages itself and an animal which disguises itself.

C 1 What presentational devices has the writer used?

2 What is the purpose of the article?

3 Who do you think is the likely audience?

VOCABULARY

Use a dictionary and the context of the passage to explain the meaning of the following words. They are underlined in the passage. The first one is done for you.

1 surroundings = *where it lives* 2 zoologists

3 technique 4 ability

5 disguise 6 resemble

SPELLING

'ist' endings

Key word: zoolog**ist**

1 Use the key word above in a sentence of your own.

2 Learn these important 'ist' words:

biolog**ist**   rac**ist**

botan**ist**   sex**ist**

chem**ist**   tour**ist**

HINT
Make sure you know the meaning of each word. Use a dictionary.

Animal camouflage

Activity / **3.2**

GRAMMAR AND PUNCTUATION

Beginning sentences

> It is important not to begin sentences in the same way every time. Writing which does this can often be boring to read.
>
> **Beginning sentences** with an 'ing' phrase is one way to add variety to your writing,
>
> eg *'**Being able to blend in with the surroundings** is a useful trick.'*

A Rewrite these sentences so that they begin with an 'ing' phrase. The first one is done for you.

1. Animals avoid predators by using camouflage.

    Using camouflage helps animals avoid predators.

2. Some animals have the ability to change colour which is very useful.

3. An Arctic fox has white fur in the winter to help it blend in with the snow.

4. A chameleon changes from bright green to dark brown to blend into its surroundings.

5. It is important for survival that the walking stick insect resembles a twig.

HINT
You may have to add or change words in your sentences.

> Another interesting way of beginning sentences is to use conjunctions,
>
> eg *'**When** snow falls in winter, its fur changes to white.'*
>
> Do not use the conjunctions 'and' or 'but' to begin sentences.

B Rewrite these sentences so that they begin with a conjunction phrase. The first one is done for you.

1. Sharks and dolphins are a blue-grey colour so they can blend in with the underwater light.

    So they can blend in with the underwater light, sharks and dolphins are a blue-grey colour.

2. The fur of the Arctic fox becomes darker after the snow has melted.

3. Deer are a brown colour because their surroundings are also brown.

4. Some animals protect themselves by using disguise.

5. The walking stick insect does not get eaten as the predator thinks it is a twig.

49

Unit 3 Reality and illusion / non-fiction

Animal camouflage

Activity / **3.2**

WRITING

Writing to inform and explain

The article 'Animal camouflage' is made up of:
- **information** about various animals
- **explanation** about camouflage.

Language features

Introduction
The first paragraph gives the reader a clear picture of what the article is about, ie
- it explains the problem: *'how to avoid being food'*
- it gives one answer: *'the art of camouflage'*.

Organisation
The writer has introduced the topic of camouflage in the first paragraph and then organised the information and explanation in three sections with subheadings:

Blending in: The natural colour of some animals makes them difficult to see in their surroundings.

Changing colour: When the surroundings change, some animals can change with it.

Disguise: Some animals can make themselves look like something else.

Tense
Usually, explanations are written in the present tense,
   eg *'One way in which nature helps animals to survive ...'*
   'The walking stick is an insect ...'

Illustrations
Explanations which appear only in text can be difficult to follow. The writer has used photographs to illustrate the various types of protection used by animals. This helps the reader to understand the explanation.

Writing assignment

Choose two of the following animals:

Research the two animals you have chosen and write an explanation of how they avoid being hunted and killed by predators. Remember, people are predators!

   tiger   cheetah   zebra

Use:
- an introductory paragraph to inform the reader what animals you are writing about
- the present tense and subheadings
- illustrations.

Unit 3 Reality and illusion / non-fiction

X-ray vision...

THE EFFECT

A spectator cuts a pack of cards into three face-down piles on the table. You gaze at the cards for a moment, then one by one you correctly name the top cards of the three piles.

THE METHOD

Before you start you must know the name of the top card on the pack. This is not difficult, just <u>glimpse</u> the card as you spread the pack, casually showing that it is ordinary (**Fig. 1**).

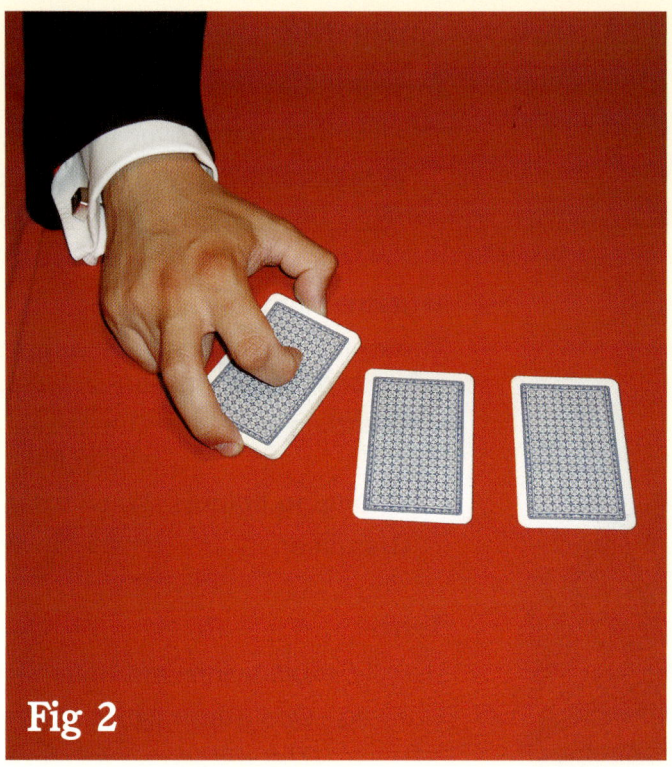

Fig 2

Fig 1

Put the pack face down on the table and ask a spectator to cut it into three roughly equal piles, keeping the cards face down. As this is being done, you must keep track of the pile with your known card on top (**Fig. 2**).

Let's say it's the Ten of Spades. You <u>announce</u> that you have X-ray vision. 'I've got enough to let me see through paper and other materials to a depth of about a millimetre. That's just deep enough to read the <u>identity</u> of a playing card.' Pause, then add, 'Sometimes.'

You point to one of the piles, not the one with the known card on top, frown for a second, then say, 'That card is the Ten of Spades.'

X-ray vision

Extract / 3.3

Fig 3

Pick up the card, without <u>revealing</u> its face (**Fig. 3**), and smile as if you were right. We will assume this card is the Three of Diamonds.

Then point to the other pile with an unknown card on top and say, 'That's the Three of Diamonds.'

Pick up the card as before (it's the King of Hearts, say), smile as you square it against the other card you hold, and point to the remaining pile.

This one has the remembered Ten of Spades on top. 'And that,' you say, 'is the King of Hearts.'

Pick up the card, smile again, and add it to the other two.

You put the cards on the table one at a time, face up, naming each one as you do (**Fig. 4**).

The effect is direct and <u>impressive</u>. You have <u>accurately</u> revealed the names of three playing cards without being able to see their faces.

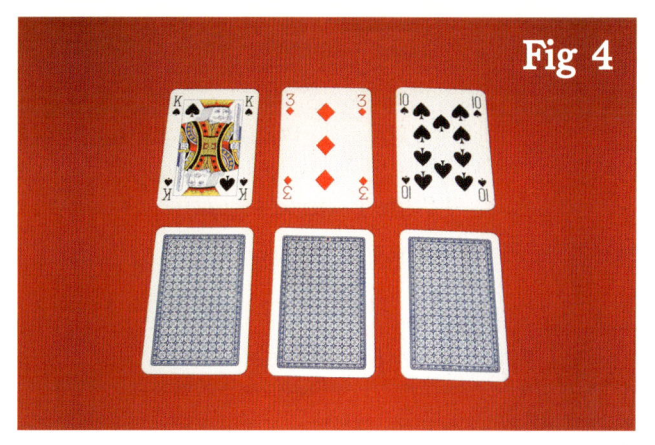

Fig 4

Card Tricks by James Weir

COMPREHENSION

A Choose the best answer for each statement.

1. For this trick, the cards have to be cut:
   a into two piles   **b** into three piles   **c** into four piles.

2. To do this trick successfully, you have to know the name of:
   a the top card in the pack   **b** the bottom card in the pack   **c** the middle card in the pack.

3. The piles must be placed on the table:
   a face up   **b** face down   **c** either way.

4. You must first point to a pile:
   a with the known card on the top   **b** with an unknown card on the top   **c** with either.

5. You will have completed the trick successfully if you can name:
   a one of the cards   **b** two of the cards   **c** all three cards.

Unit 3 Reality and illusion / non-fiction

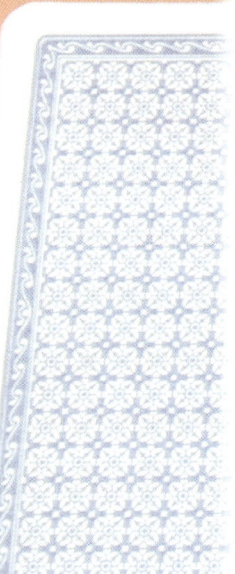

B 1 Explain the following in your own words:
   a *'cuts a pack of cards'*
   b *'keep track of'*
   c *'X-ray vision'*.

2 Why do you think you are told not to pick up the known card first?

3 Why do you think the instructions tell you to *'Pause'*, *'smile'* and *'frown for a second'*?

4 How helpful / unhelpful did you find the photographs? If you could add another photograph, what part of the trick would you illustrate?

C Follow the instructions and do the trick.
- Did it work?
- Did you find the instructions easy / difficult to follow?
- What would you add to the instructions to make it easier to do the trick?

VOCABULARY

Use a dictionary and the context of the passage to explain the meaning of the following words. They are underlined in the instructions. The first one is done for you

1 glimpse = look quickly at
2 announce
3 identity
4 revealing
5 impressive
6 accurately

SPELLING

'se' words

Key word: pau**se**

1 Use the key word above in a sentence of your own.

2 Learn these important **'se'** words:

clau**se**   endor**se**

cour**se**   recompen**se**

disea**se**   sen**se**

HINT
Be careful! 'ce' makes the same sound as some of these 'se' words.

X-ray vision

Activity / **3.3**

GRAMMAR AND PUNCTUATION

Imperative verbs

> **Remember!** A **verb** is an action or being word,
> eg action: You **gaze** at the cards
>   being: I **am** impressed
>
> An **imperative verb** is used to give instructions or orders. An imperative verb uses the verb family name, dropping the word 'to',
>
> eg **Verb family name**   imperative
>   to put   put
>   to pick   pick

A Write the imperative verb in each sentence. The first one is done for you.

1 Shuffle the cards.   *shuffle*
2 Glimpse the top card as you show the spectators the pack.
3 Smile as you name the card.
4 After that, point to the next pile.
5 Say, 'That card is the Ten of Spades.'

B Change these sentences so that they begin with an imperative verb. The first one is done for you.

1 Would you please shuffle the cards for me.
   Shuffle the cards for me please.
2 Can you choose a card from the pack.
3 I would like you to put the card face down on the table.
4 I want you to think about the card you have chosen.
5 Now will you pick up the card.

> The **negative imperative** uses 'don't' meaning do not,
> eg **Imperative**   **Negative imperative**
>   deal (the cards)   don't deal (the cards)

C Use these negative imperatives in sentences of your own.

1 don't look
2 don't guess
3 don't tell

Unit 3 Reality and illusion / non-fiction

X-ray vision

Activity / **3.3**

WRITING

Instructions

> 'X-ray vision' is a set of **instructions** explaining how to perform a card trick. It uses:
> - simple language
> - imperative verbs
> - illustrations in the form of photographs.

Language features

Structure

The instructions have to be followed in order to do the trick successfully. The writer has not numbered the instructions but has set out the paragraphs in blocks so that it is easy to see where one instruction ends and another begins,

   eg *'You point to one of the piles ...'*   *'Pick up the card ...'*

Imperative verbs

Imperative verbs are used in instructions and orders,

   eg '**Put** *the pack face down*'   '**Pick up** *the card*'

Style

Usually instructions tell you what to **do**. As these are instructions for a trick which will be performed in front of an audience, the writer includes instructions which tell you:
- what to **say**, eg *'That's the Three of Diamonds'*
- how to **act**, eg *'frown for a second'*

Illustrations

It is often easier to follow instructions if they are illustrated. The illustrations can be drawings, photographs or diagrams. The photographs in 'X-ray vision' help you to 'see' the position of the cards at various stages of the trick.

Writing assignment

Think of a simple trick that you know. It may be a card trick or a trick where you make something 'disappear'.

Write a set of clear instructions for the trick, using imperative verbs and illustrations.

Remember to tell the reader:
- what to do
- what to say
- how to act.

Unit 4 We are the champions / non-fiction

the icing on the cake...

They could not have explained the offside rule to save their lives. They would rather spend Saturday afternoon in a super-market or a science park than a football stadium. Yet on Sunday 31 July 1966, millions of people in England woke up having <u>acquired</u> the curious ability to recite 11 names: Banks, Cohen, Wilson, Stiles, Charlton J, Moore, Ball, Hunt, Charlton R, Hurst and Peters ... England, for the first time, had won the football World Cup at Wembley Stadium on

England win the World Cup

Extract / **4.1**

Saturday 30 July and in doing so they had put the icing on the cake of a delicious, triumphant and, yes, very British, decade.

The importance of what was to happen at Wembley could be measured on the streets of England, if not of Britain (in Scotland, certainly, people determinedly went about other business, or claimed to be doing so). English streets were all but empty. Buses travelled their usual routes, but the driver was also the only passenger. Shops either installed television sets or closed down for the duration. Patrolling police officers somehow found their attention drawn to the windows of shops that sold televisions, shops which became, for two hours, the most guarded in the country.

The television audience, worldwide, was 400 million, their pictures delivered by the BBC. They saw a final that was not as great as it is sometimes painted, though it was certainly dramatic. Germany went ahead, England equalised, England went ahead, Germany equalised seconds from the end of normal time. Then, in the extra half hour, two more goals from England, the first hotly disputed but awarded after a lengthy conversation between a referee from Switzerland and a linesman from Azerbaijan. The final score: 4-2. The last goal was accompanied, for television viewers, by what is perhaps the most famous piece of commentary in sporting history. The BBC commentator, Kenneth Wolstenholme, saw Geoff Hurst collect the ball inside the German half but noticed, out of the corner of an eye, that a few English fans were approaching the pitch, anticipating the final whistle. Hurst strode forward with the ball, into the left side of the German penalty area. 'Some people are on the pitch,' Wolstenholme said, 'they think it's all over ...'. Hurst ignored little Alan Ball, who was galloping into the penalty area and screaming for a pass, and instead lashed a glorious, rising shot past Tilowski, the German goalkeeper; '... it is now' Wolstenholme said.

A fairy-tale. The country that invented football had at last contrived to win the World Cup, which had been played every four years, outside of wartime, since 1930.

We Interrupt This Programme –
20 News Stories That Marked a Century
by Peter Barnard

COMPREHENSION

A Copy these sentences. Fill in the missing words.

1 England won the World Cup on _ _ _ _ _ _ _ _ , 30 July 1966.
2 Police officers watched the match through shop _ _ _ _ _ _ _.
3 400 _ _ _ _ _ _ _ people, worldwide, watched the game.
4 Keith Wolstenholme was the BBC _ _ _ _ _ _ _ _ _ _ _.
5 Geoff _ _ _ _ _ scored the final goal.

Unit 4 We are the champions / non-fiction

B 1 Explain the following in your own words:
  a 'put the icing on the cake'
  b 'hotly disputed'
  c 'a fairy-tale'.

2 Why do you think Scotland was not interested in the World Cup final?

3 What do you think the writer means when he says that the final 'was not as great as it is sometimes painted'?

4 Why do you think that Hurst did not pass the ball to Alan Ball?

C Do you think the writer:
- likes football
- does not like football?

Quote from the article to support your answer.

VOCABULARY

Use a dictionary and the context of the extract to explain the meaning of the following words. They are underlined in the passage. The first one is done for you.

1 acquired = *gained*
2 installed
3 duration
4 painted
5 anticipating
6 contrived

SPELLING

'tch' words

Key word: pi**tch**

1 Use the key word above in a sentence of your own.

2 Learn these important '**tch**' words:

crossha**tch**   ske**tch**

ma**tch**   sti**tch**

pa**tch**   wa**tch**

HINT

Make sure you know the meaning of each word. Use a dictionary.

60

England win the World Cup

Activity / **4.1**

GRAMMAR AND PUNCTUATION

Adverbial clauses

> **Remember!** Complex sentences are made up of:
> - a main clause = makes sense on its own
> - a second clause = does not make sense on its own.
>
> The second clause is also called a subordinate clause. Sometimes:
> - the subordinate clause does the same job as an adverb
> - it tells us when, why or how the action was done
> - it is called an **adverbial clause**.
>
> <u>England won the World Cup</u> <u>when Hurst scored the final goal</u>.
>   main clause   adverbial clause
>
> Adverbial clauses may begin with a conjunction, which shows that the action depends on what happened before: words like *when*, *if* and *although*.

A Copy these sentences, underlining the adverbial clauses. The first one is done for you.

1. When Germany went ahead, England responded with an equaliser.

   <u>When Germany went ahead</u>, England responded with an equaliser.

2. The referee awarded the goal after a lengthy conversation with the linesman.

3. Geoff Hurst ignored little Alan Ball when he was galloping into the penalty area.

4. The game was like a fairy-tale because England won the World Cup.

> **HINT**
> Sometimes the adverbial clause comes at the beginning!

B Add an adverbial clause to each sentence to make it more interesting and informative. Use the conjunctions in the box.

| before | so | when | because |

1. Saturday 30 July 1966 was an important day.
2. No one travelled on the buses.
3. 400 million people watched the television.
4. Police officers stood outside television shops.
5. Some English fans went onto the pitch.
6. The match was over.

61

Unit 4 We are the champions / non-fiction

England win the World Cup

Activity / **4.1**

WRITING

Writing to inform and entertain

> 'England win the World Cup' is one of a collection of articles which appear in a book entitled *We Interrupt This Programme – 20 News Stories That Marked a Century*. The purpose of the book is to inform its readers, in an entertaining way, about the most important events of the twentieth century.

Language features

Factual information

As with all writing to inform, facts about the subject must be included,

eg *'England, for the first time, had won the football World Cup at Wembley Stadium on Saturday 30 July ...'*
    'a referee from Switzerland'

Descriptive detail

The writer of this article cannot be mysterious or surprise his readers as he is writing about a well-known event. To make it interesting and vivid for readers he uses descriptive detail which brings the event alive,

eg *'hotly disputed ...'*
    'lashed a glorious, rising shot ...'

Entertaining the reader

The writer uses humour to entertain the readers. He finds it amusing that:

- people who had no interest in football could *'recite 11 names'* – those of the winning England football team
- police officers suddenly thought it was very important to guard television shops!

Writing assignment

Choose an event which you have witnessed at your school. You could choose a sporting event or a play, or think of your own idea.

Write an article for a local newspaper which both informs and entertains your readers.

You should include:

- factual information
- descriptive detail
- some humour.

63

Unit 4 We are the champions / non-fiction

Taylor-made passport to the world

The Great Britain team has home advantage, a new captain, much more experience on grass – and a victory is a must, says *Julian Muscat*

Different captain, different venue, same goal.
Davis Cup tennis returns this weekend when Great Britain take on Ecuador at the game's most famous venue. When the Wimbledon gates open on Friday, fans will cheer a team captained for the first time by Roger Taylor, thrice Wimbledon semi-finalist and a Davis Cup stalwart three decades ago.

Taylor-made passport to the world

Extract / **4.2**

No 1 Court should resemble the cockpit of noise that has served Great Britain so well over recent ties in Birmingham. Victory is a must: the losers will be <u>relegated</u> from the 16-nation World Group and into that tennis wasteland from which Britain has only recently emerged.

The tie offers Tim Henman and Greg Rusedski a perfect opportunity to bounce back from disappointing efforts at Wimbledon and to reinstate themselves in the nation's hearts. The venue has been chosen to <u>maximise</u> Britain's prospects: both Henman and Rusedski excel on grass, a surface on which Nicolas Lappentti, Ecuador's star turn, has little experience …

Taylor is under no illusions about the importance of the tie. 'It is a showcase for British tennis, a little like Wimbledon,' he says. 'It is very important that we compete at the highest level. That's why this match against Ecuador is so important.'

He believes that the Davis Cup gives a whole new audience a chance to watch tennis in a different atmosphere. 'It is unique,' he says. 'You're not just supporting a player, you're supporting Great Britain. We, as a team, are playing for Great Britain. Hopefully, there will be kids with their faces painted, waving flags and banners and blowing horns. We are all looking forward to it.'

Taylor, who is 58, assumed his new role after the dismissal of David Lloyd, the previous captain, earlier this year. His first move was to appoint Jeremy Bates, director of men's tennis at the Lawn Tennis Association, as team coach.

This weekend will give Taylor his first taste of Davis Cup tennis outside of playing, of which he has great memories, such as his Davis Cup <u>debut</u>, away to Hungary on clay in 1966. With the tie poised at 2-2, Taylor won the decisive rubber by beating Istvan Gulyas, who had only recently reached the final of the French Open, where he lost to Tony Roche.

'One of my best memories of playing Davis Cup,' Taylor reflects, 'is the <u>camaraderie</u> that develops between players – especially in away matches, when there are not that many people supporting you. I think one of the most important things is to build team spirit.'

COMPREHENSION

A Write 'true' or 'false' for each of these statements.

1 Great Britain is playing against Hungary.
2 They are playing at Wimbledon.
3 The captain of the British team is Roger Taylor.
4 The British players are Rusedski and Roach.
5 When Taylor was playing tennis against Hungary he won the tie.

Unit 4 We are the champions / non-fiction

B 1 Explain the following in your own words:
  a *'victory is a must'*
  b *'excel on grass'*
  c *'under no illusions'*.

2 How is Davis Cup tennis different from other tennis matches?

3 Why do you think the writer included Taylor's success as a tennis player in the Davis Cup?

4 Explain in your own words why winning against Ecuador is so important.

C What do you think is Taylor's attitude to the Davis Cup? Quote from the text to support your impressions.

You should consider:
- his quotes
- what is written about him.

VOCABULARY

Use a dictionary and the context of the extract to explain the meaning of the following words. They are underlined in the passage. The first one is done for you.

1 venue = *place*
2 stalwart
3 relegated
4 maximise
5 debut
6 camaraderie

SPELLING

Words ending in 'ory'

Key word: vict**ory**

1 Use the key word above in a sentence of your own.

2 Learn these important '**ory**' words:

explanat**ory**   mem**ory**

hist**ory**   satisfact**ory**

laborat**ory**   territ**ory**

> **HINT**
> Most 'ory' nouns make their plural with 'ies', eg memor**y** – memor**ies**.

Taylor-made passport to the world

Activity / **4.2**

GRAMMAR AND PUNCTUATION

Complex sentences

> **Remember:**
> - A **complex sentence** is made up of one main clause and one or more subordinate clauses.
> - Subordinate clauses cannot make sense on their own.
>
>   eg *Davis Cup tennis returns this weekend* — main clause
>   *when Great Britain takes on Ecuador.* — subordinate clause
>
> '*when Great Britain takes on Ecuador*' does not make sense on its own.

A Copy these complex sentences and underline the main clause in red. Highlight the subordinate clauses or underline them in a different colour. The first one is done for you.

1. Fans will cheer the team when they step onto the court.
   <u>Fans will cheer the team</u> <u>when they step onto the court</u>.
2. Grass was chosen as it will favour the Great Britain team.
3. Taylor won the decisive rubber when he beat Gulyas.
4. Britain need to win so they will not be relegated.

> Subordinate clauses can come first in a **complex** sentence,
>
>   eg <u>When they step onto the court</u> , <u>fans will cheer the team.</u>
>   subordinate clause   comma   main clause

B Rewrite the sentences in **A**, putting the subordinate clause first.

C Add a subordinate clause to each sentence to make it more interesting and informative.

1. Great Britain could win this tournament.
2. Greg Rusedski has been unlucky this year.
3. There are many talented young players.
4. Children should have opportunities to play tennis.

Unit 4 We are the champions / non-fiction

Taylor-made passport to the world

Activity / **4.2**

WRITING

Newspaper articles

> 'Taylor-made passport to the world' is an article which appeared in a free Davis Cup newspaper which was given to everyone as they arrived at the event at Wimbledon.

Language features

The audience

The writer knows that most of the people reading this article will understand the game of tennis. He feels no need to explain everything because he expects that his audience will have the necessary background knowledge,

- eg *'the 16-nation World Group'*
  'the decisive rubber'

Tenses

Most newspaper articles are written in the past tense about events which have already happened. This article is different because part of it is about what is going to happen, so the future tense is used,

eg	**Past tense**	**Future tense**
	*'the venue **has been chosen**'*	*'fans **will cheer** a team captained'*
	*'Taylor ... **assumed** his new role'*	*'there **will be** kids'*

Use of quotes

The writer has interviewed Roger Taylor so that he can report 'from the horse's mouth',

- eg *'It is a showcase for British tennis ...'*
  'One of my best memories of playing Davis Cup ...'

Writing assignment

Choose a real or imaginary international sporting event which is to take place this coming weekend and write a newspaper article which:

- explains the event and its importance
- gives information about the two teams
- speculates about the likely outcome
- includes quotes from key people.

You must decide on:

- the intended purpose of the article
- the intended audience.

Unit 4 We are the champions / non-fiction

...the way it is...

On 4 September 1992 Tanni Grey-Thompson broke the record for the 400 metres in a wheelchair. Since then she has won many medals and marathons. This is how it all began.

I've never thought why me? I've never cried because I'm in a wheelchair and I've never felt bitter. This is just the way it is. People feel sorry for me and <u>assume</u> I've got a sad, tragic life because they don't look past the chair. But if it doesn't bother me why should it bother anyone? One day, when I was little, I was sitting on the kitchen floor and my mum asked me what I thought about having spina bifida. I said, 'Well, if it wasn't me then it would be someone else. I've got it, there's nothing I can do about it, so I might as well get on with it.' That's always been my <u>attitude</u>.

I don't remember a time when I wasn't involved in sport. Like most kids, I started off by doing stuff at junior school – rounders, netball and little PE lessons. When I moved up to St Cyres, I wasn't allowed to stay in mainstream school for PE. I was meant to go back to the special school but I didn't like it because I didn't know most of the kids. They were doing daft things like musical movement and pretending to be trees. I hated it.

Seize the day!

Extract / 4.3

I wanted to do the good stuff!

The mainstream school had a swimming pool. One day when I was eleven I was watching the kids swim and the PE teacher, Mrs Gogbill, saw me. I wasn't meant to be there and she was a very scary woman. I was constantly terrified of her. She looked at me carefully and then said, 'Have you got a swimming costume?'

'Yes,' I croaked.

'Well, bring it next week and get in the pool.'

So I started swimming a lot. I'd already learnt how to swim at junior school. Mr Thomas's attitude was that children had to learn to swim and there was never an issue of me not being allowed to go on the weekly trips to the pool. Mum would come with me to help me change and I remember the instructor, who always called me 'Chick', pushing me out into the water on the rescue pole and telling me to let go. I did and flailed around, doing a pretty pathetic doggy paddle, to get to the side. Eventually I did a length and remember sinking lower and lower in the water the further I went, but feeling fantastic when I'd done it.

It was difficult at secondary school because the sports I liked were things like tennis. At the time wheelchair tennis wasn't very well developed and it was hard to compete against non-disabled children. But then there was a sports day at special school and I went to that. I didn't want to compete against other people in wheelchairs, but it got me off French, so I went. To my surprise I really enjoyed it. There was stuff like the 60 metres, cricket ball throwing and the slalom. We weren't allowed anything dangerous like discuses because we were from the special school, but it was a good day where you charged around and did lots of different things. I won a few medals, including the 60 metres. Dad's still got the certificates. After that I kept doing more and more.

I don't remember making a conscious decision that I was going to do athletics and nothing else …

Seize the Day! by Tanni Grey-Thompson

COMPREHENSION

A Choose the best answer for each statement.

1 Tanni began playing sport at:
   a nursery school
   b junior school
   c secondary school.

2 She had to go back to the special school for:
   a maths
   b French
   c PE.

3 She was allowed to swim at junior school by:
   a her Mum
   b Mr Thomas
   c Mrs Gogbill.

4 Going to the special school sports day meant she didn't have to do:
   a French
   b musical movement
   c tennis.

5 She won a medal in the:
   a 100 metre race
   b 200 metre race
   c 60 metre race.

Unit 4 We are the champions / non-fiction

B 1 Explain the following in your own words:
  a *'they don't look past the chair'*
  b *'mainstream school'*
  c *'constantly terrified of her'*.

  2 Who do you think Mr Thomas was?

  3 In what ways do you imagine Tanni found it hard *'to compete against non-disabled children'*?

  4 How do you know that Tanni's dad was very proud of her?

C What impression to you get of Tanni Grey-Thompson from the extract?
  You should consider:
  - her attitude to her disability
  - her attitude to sport
  - her life at school.

VOCABULARY

Use a dictionary and the context of the extract to explain the meaning of the following words. They are underlined in the passage. The first one is done for you.

1 assume = think
2 attitude
3 flailed
4 pathetic
5 slalom
6 conscious

SPELLING

Words ending in 'ise' / 'yse'

Key word: surpr**ise**

  1 Use the key word above in a sentence of your own.

  2 Learn these important **'ise'** / **'yse'** words:

  adv**ise**   improv**ise**

  analy**se**   prioriti**se**

  dramati**se** reali**se**

> **HINT**
> Make sure you know the meaning of each word. Use a dictionary.

Seize the day!

Activity / **4.3**

GRAMMAR AND PUNCTUATION

Joining sentences – semi-colons

> This is a **semi-colon** ;
>
> It is used to separate items in a **list** of statements in a sentence,
>
> eg *Tanni didn't like PE in the special school; she didn't like musical movement; and she hated pretending to be a tree.*

A Copy the sentences and add the semi-colons. The first one is done for you.

1. Tanni didn't mind being in a wheelchair she never cried she didn't feel bitter and she never felt sorry for herself.

   Tanni didn't mind being in a wheelchair; she never cried; she didn't feel bitter; and she never felt sorry for herself.

2. When Tanni was in the swimming pool she enjoyed herself she flailed around did doggy paddle and managed to swim a length of the pool.

3. Sports day was fun there was a 60 metre race throwing the cricket ball and competing in the slalom.

> A semi-colon is also used to separate two statements in a sentence which balance each other.
>
> [1] *Tanni hated musical movement;* [2] *she loved swimming.*
>
> Statement 1: what she hated
> Statement 2: what she loved

B Copy the sentences and add the semi-colons. The first one has been done for you.

1. Tanni was interested in sport she was not interested in French.

   Tanni was interested in sport; she was not interested in French.

2. She enjoyed the sports day she won a few medals.

3. Her Dad was very proud of her he kept the certificates.

Unit 4 We are the champions / non-fiction

Seize the day!

Activity / **4.3**

WRITING

Autobiography

> *Seize the Day!* is Tanni Grey-Thompson's **autobiography**.
> It tells us some facts about her life and how she felt.

Language features

Factual details

Obviously, when someone writes about their life, they include factual information,

  eg *'I'd already learnt how to swim at junior school.'*

Feelings and reflections

Along with the factual details of her life, the writer lets the reader see how she felt about things as she looks back over her life to date,

  eg *'They were doing things like musical movement and pretending to be trees. I hated it. I wanted to do the good stuff.'*

Style

The writer has adopted a very 'chatty', informal style. It is as if she is speaking directly to the reader and gives the impression of a very 'normal', down-to-earth person,

  eg *'Mum would come with me ...'*   *'... but it got me off French ...'*

Tense

As the writer is writing about things that have already happened, she uses the past tense,

  eg *'I was watching the kids swim ...'*   *' I did a length ...'*

Writing assignment

Imagine you are a world record holder in a sport of your choice. Write an autobiographical extract which:

- explains how you became interested in your sport
- recounts the actual event where you broke the world record.

Remember to:

- include your thoughts and feelings as well as the facts
- write in an informal style
- use the past tense.

Unit 5 Rebel with a cause / *non-fiction*

The origin of Cool

It is nearly the 40th anniversary of James Dean's death and his popularity is as great as ever.

James Dean was little more than a boy when he died, killed at twenty-four on the highway near Paso Robles, California, on 30 September 1955, while on his way to a sports car meet. At the time of his death, Dean had completed three movies, *East of Eden*, *Rebel Without a Cause*, and *Giant*, only the first of which had been released. Dean was already an actor of promise, and his death was front-page news. It was ... a time of peace and prosperity when young people were expected to respect their elders and obey the rules. But even during his short life, Dean was widely known as a nonconformist – a rebel who had taken Hollywood by storm and who did as he pleased. For young people coming of age, Dean was someone they could easily identify with: an outsider, a loner – he was the antithesis of everything a well-behaved youth was supposed to be.

The Origin of Cool

Extract / 5.1

His screen portrayals symbolised the rebelliousness of adolescence. In public he was often rude, even surly. A fan magazine quoted him as saying, 'I wouldn't like me, if I had to be around me.' He had been known to fight with directors and storm off the set. 'Jimmy knew what young people were up against,' an admirer once said. 'He understood.' Later, someone else referred to him as 'the first student activist'.

From the day of his death, it seemed that young people would not let Dean die. A special fan mail agency had to deal with the <u>deluge</u> of mail that poured into the studio. Many of the letters were addressed to the dead star.

A record, *His Name Was Dean*, put out on a small label, sold twenty-five thousand copies in a single week. Mattson's, a Hollywood clothing shop, received hundreds of orders for red jackets identical to the one Dean had worn in *Rebel Without a Cause*, and Griffith Park, where scenes from the movie were shot, became almost overnight a tourist attraction. Admirers lined up inside the Observatory, hoping to sit in the same seat Dean had used in the film …

Some fans refused to believe that Dean was really dead. Walter Winchell printed in his column the rumour that Dean was disfigured but still alive. Other stories insisted that it had been a hitchhiker and not Dean who had been killed and that the actor was in hiding while learning to operate his artificial limbs or that he had been placed in a <u>sanatorium</u>.

Not everyone, however, was enthusiastic about Dean. Herbert Mitgang, of *The New York Times*, dismissed him as 'an honour graduate of the black leather jacket and motorcycle school of acting and living it up.' And director Elia Kazan, Dean's mentor, claimed: 'Every boy goes through a period when he's seventeen or so when he hates his father, hates authority, can't live within the rules … It's a classic case. Dean just never got out of it.' …

Humphrey Bogart, who also knew a thing or two about image making, once said: 'Dean died at just the right time. He left behind a legend. If he had lived, he'd never have been able to live up to his publicity.'

But Dean did not live and in death became transformed into a myth: even today, visitors come from all over to visit his grave in Fairmount, Indiana, the small farming community where Dean grew up. In one recent year, there were over six thousand visitors, some from as far away as Argentina and Australia. Dean's handsome, brooding face adorns posters and T-shirts. A licensing company, run by lawyers, markets James Dean calendars, postcards, and ashtrays around the world.

Rebel for All Seasons by Ron Martinetti

COMPREHENSION

A   Copy these sentences. Fill in the missing words.

1   James Dean died at the age of __ __ __ __ __ __ __ __ __ __.

2   He had made only __ __ __ __ __ films before his death.

3   Rumours said that it was a __ __ __ __ __ __ __ __ __ who died in the car crash.

4   James Dean is buried in __ __ __ __ __ __ __ __ __, Indiana.

5   People come from as far away as Argentina and __ __ __ __ __ __ __ __ __ to visit his grave.

Unit 5 Rebel with a cause / non-fiction

B 1 Explain the following in your own words:
  a *'an actor of promise'*
  b *'taken Hollywood by storm'*
  c *'living it up'*.

2 Give two examples of how his fans *'would not let Dean die'*.

3 What do you think Humphrey Bogart meant when he said that if Dean had lived *'he'd never have been able to live up to his publicity'*?

4 Explain why you think James Dean was so popular with young people.

C Find evidence in the text which shows that:
- James Dean was very popular
- not everyone thought he was wonderful.

VOCABULARY

Use a dictionary and the context of the passage to explain the meaning of the following words. They are underlined in the passage. The first one is done for you.

1 meet = *meeting / gathering*
2 prosperity
3 nonconformist
4 antithesis
5 deluge
6 sanatorium

SPELLING

Double 'n' words

Key word: **ann**iversary

1 Use the key word above in a sentence of your own.

2 Learn these important **double 'n'** words:

a**nn**ual   pla**nn**ing

begi**nn**ing   questio**nn**aire

i**nn**ocent   sca**nn**er

HINT
*Remember to double an 'n' after a short vowel when adding 'ing / ed / er' eg run – ru**nn**ing.*

The origin of Cool

Activity / **5.1**

GRAMMAR AND PUNCTUATION

Pronouns

> A **pronoun** is a word that can be used instead of a noun,
> eg 'Dean was already an actor of promise ...'
> noun   pronoun
> **He** was already an actor of promise ...
>
> Using pronouns means we can avoid repetition,
> eg James Dean was little more than a boy when James Dean died.
> 'James Dean was little more than a boy when **he** died.'

A Copy the sentences. Replace the underlined nouns with a suitable pronoun. The first one is done for you.

1 The film was called 'Rebel Without a Cause'.

It was called 'Rebel Without a Cause'.

2 Young people would not let Dean die.

3 Walter Winchell thought Dean was still alive.

4 A record sold twenty-five thousand copies in a week.

5 Fans came to Dean's grave from all over the world.

> Some **pronouns** tell us who 'owns' something,
> eg '**his** death was front-page news'.
> '**his**' is a possessive pronoun.

B Copy the sentences. Replace the underlined words with a possessive pronoun from the box. The first one is done for you.

mine   its   theirs   ours   hers

1 The photograph of James Dean is my sister's.

The photograph of James Dean is hers.

2 This video 'Giant' is my video.

3 James Dean's death was the newspaper's front page story.

4 These red jackets are the fans' red jackets.

5 Those T-shirts are our T-shirts.

79

Unit 5 Rebel with a cause / non-fiction

The origin of Cool

Activity / **5.1**

WRITING

For and against

> The writer of *Rebel for All Seasons* has researched the subject of James Dean and presented evidence to show that:
> - some people were very enthusiastic about the actor – **for**
> - some people were not very enthusiastic about the actor – **against**.

Language features

Background information

Some people reading this article about James Dean will already know a lot about him. Other readers will not. The writer helps the readers who do not know much about James Dean by giving some information about him,

   eg He died *'on 30 September 1955'*   *'In public he was often rude, even surly.'*

Opinions

So was James Dean a wonderful actor or not? The writer has included various opinions,

   eg **for:** *'For young people ... Dean was someone they could easily identify with.'*
           'Some fans refused to believe that Dean was really dead.'
   against: *'He had been known to fight with directors and storm off the set.'*
           'Herbert Mitgang, of The New York Times, dismissed him ...'

Quotations

The writer uses quotes from people who had an opinion about Dean,

   eg **for:** *' "Jimmy knew what young people were up against," an admirer once said.'*
   against: *'an honour graduate of the black leather jacket and motorcycle school of acting and living it up'*

Anecdotes

These are short accounts about incidents which help the reader understand what Dean was like,

   eg *'A fan magazine quoted him as saying, "I wouldn't like me, if I had to be around me." '*

Writing assignment

Choose an actor, singer or sports personality who you are interested in. Research the person you have chosen and write an article about him / her. Include:
- background information
- reasons why some people like and admire him / her
- reasons why some people dislike him / her.

Unit 5 Rebel with a cause / non-fiction

We shall not be moved...

Forms of protest

Through the centuries, people have used various forms of protest to show that they disagree with a particular situation. Workers have protested about how they are treated by their employers; people have protested about how they are governed by their local councils and parliament. Sometimes a protest happens spontaneously but more often, protests are carefully planned to get as much attention as possible.

Forms of protest

Extract / 5.2

The Luddites

In the early years of the nineteenth century, workers in the north of England found themselves in a difficult situation. They worked in textile mills where cloth and garments were produced by hand. Their wages were lowered and their jobs threatened with the invention of machines that could do the work more quickly and economically. A group of workers decided to protest. They broke into factories in Nottingham and destroyed the new machines. This form of protest spread to Yorkshire, Lancashire, Leicestershire and Derbyshire. Special constables were sent to protect the factories.

In 1812, Parliament passed the Frame Breaking Law. Anyone caught destroying machines would be sentenced to death. In that year, eight men were executed in Lancashire and 13 transported to Australia. Another 15 were executed in York.

Sit-ins

This type of protest was very popular in the 1960s in America. Groups of people just sat down on the pavement, in parks and in shops, and refused to move. The protesters' aims were to cause as much disruption as possible and to get the public's attention for their grievances. The police often had to use dogs and water hoses to get the protesters to move.

As sit-ins were a form of non-violent protest, the pictures of protesters being drenched or carried off into police vans aroused public sympathy.

At this time, the Civil Rights Movement was formed to persuade the government that black people should have equal rights with white people. The first sit-in happened in Greensboro, North Carolina on 1 February 1960. Four black schoolboys went into Woolworths, sat down at the lunch counter and asked for coffee. As they were black, they were refused service so they refused to move. The next day, 29 more people joined them and on 3 February, 63 of the 65 seats at the lunch counter were occupied by students protesting about how black people were treated. On 4 February, three white women joined the sit-in and by 5 February, there were more than 300 protesters. In two months the sit-in movement had spread to 54 cities and the government had to take notice.

COMPREHENSION

A Write 'true' or 'false' for each of these statements.

1. People protest to show that they disagree with something.
2. The Luddites were special constables.
3. The Frame Breaking Law was passed in 1812.
4. People joining sit-ins were very violent.
5. The first sit-in happened in Yorkshire.

Unit 5   Rebel with a cause / non-fiction

B 1 Explain the following in your own words:
   a *'through the centuries'*
   b *'non-violent protest'*
   c *'aroused public sympathy'*.

   2 Explain in your own words why people protest.

   3 What do you think the Luddites hoped to achieve by breaking the machines?

   4 What do you think of sit-ins as a form of protest?

C Copy and complete the chart about the Greensboro sit-in.

Date	Event
1 February 1960	Four black school boys were refused service at the Woolworths lunch counter. They refused to move.
2 February 1960	
3 February 1960	
4 February 1960	
5 February 1960	

VOCABULARY

Use a dictionary and the context of the passage to explain the meaning of the following words. They are underlined in the passage. The first one is done for you.

1 threatened = *in danger*   2 economically   3 transported

4 disruption   5 grievances   6 occupied

SPELLING

'eous' words

Key word: spontan**eous**

1 Use the key word above in a sentence of your own.

2 Learn these important **'eous'** words:

court**eous**   outrag**eous**

hid**eous**   right**eous**

miscellan**eous**   simultan**eous**

> **HINT**
> *Make sure you know the meaning of these words. Use a dictionary.*

Forms of protest

Activity / **5.2**

GRAMMAR AND PUNCTUATION

Some common mistakes

> You can avoid some **common mistakes** by thinking very carefully about:
> 1 the correct spelling
> 2 the correct part of speech
> 3 correct punctuation.

A Copy the sentences using the correct word from the brackets.

1 In the point-to-point race, you have to ride back and (fourth / forth) from (hear / here) to (their / there).
2 (Your / You're) about to (loose / lose) (your / you're) place in the queue.
3 Everyone will (expect / except) you (two / to / too) (accept / except) the prize.
4 Do you know (weather / whether) or (knot / not) (you'll / Yule) be able to come to the party?
5 Many people (choose / chose) to live in the countryside because of the pollution of the cities.
6 Did (yew / you) get (through / thorough / threw) your interview without stammering?
7 What did the careers officer (advice / advise) you to do? Did you take her (advice / advise)?
8 (There / Their / They're) are (alot / a lot) of (your / you're) friends on the trip to Venice.

B Use these words in sentences of your own.

1 beside
2 besides
3 borrow
4 lend
5 bought
6 brought

Unit 5 Rebel with a cause / non-fiction

Forms of protest

Activity / **5.2**

WRITING
Writing to inform

> The article 'Forms of protest' is a piece of non-fiction writing to **inform** readers about ways in which people have protested through the ages.

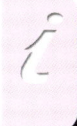

Language features

Main heading

The main heading tells the reader exactly what the article is about, ie

Forms of protest

Subheadings

These are used to divide up the information so that the reader can concentrate on one thing at a time, ie

The Luddites
Sit-ins

Style

Information texts should be written in a formal style, not a chatty one, eg
Formal style:

- often uses the passive voice   eg *'the Civil Rights Movement was formed'*
- does not use contractions   eg *'how they are (they're) treated'*
- uses specialist vocabulary   eg *'Luddites' 'Frame Breaking Law'*

Facts

The writer has researched the subject and presented the facts,

eg *'They broke into factories in Nottingham ...'*
    'Greensboro, North Carolina on 1 February 1960'

Writing assignment

Another form of protest is the protest march. Research one of these groups:

- CND – People who protest about the manufacture and use of nuclear weapons.
- Animal Rights – People who protest about the use of animals for experiments.
- The Countryside Alliance – People who want the way of life in the countryside to remain unchanged. They have protested about the ban on fox hunting.

Write an article to inform readers where, when and why your chosen group has staged a protest march.

Unit 5 Rebel with a cause / non-fiction

petty rules...

Anne Robinson went to a boarding school at Farnborough Hill. Immediately she arrived, she began to find ways of avoiding things she didn't want to do!

I always wanted to go to boarding school. I had always been at a convent school but I had read a lot of Angela Brazil and the Twins at Mallory Towers – or were they St Clare's? Anyway, I just thought it would be very exciting to go to a convent boarding school. In fact, it didn't really live up to my expectations although it was still exciting to be away from home and on my own. I had a brother who had gone to boarding school, so it seemed to me that I should be doing exactly the same.

I learnt very little during my time there in terms of academic achievement. I really didn't do anything. I got a few 'O' levels; but what I really learnt a great deal about was survival and bucking the system, about

Something About A Convent Girl

Extract / **5.3**

being <u>devious</u> and never giving up. There was always a way round everything because convent life was made up, for the large part, of a lot of <u>inexplicable</u>, petty rules. They seemed to me to be petty rules, so you had to decide how best you could stay there with <u>credibility</u> but not do what they wanted you to do.

One of the particularly petty rules was that the new headmistress decided that all post must be opened unless it was from our parents. This was tricky because I had fallen deeply in love with a boy at my brother's school, Ampleforth. The highlight of term time was that he wrote to me. It was all very innocent but I was blowed if I wanted Mother Rosemary Alexander to have a look at his letters first. I asked my parents to address twenty or thirty envelopes to me at the beginning of term and then I gave them to him. That way none of his post was opened on its way to me. Now that was a prime example of how they got you into a bit of lateral thinking. Mind you, you need <u>liberal</u> parents! ...

I never went through a religious period. I prayed quite often for it to be the end of term but that was it. I spent a lot of time being locked up because I was <u>opinionated</u> at school and I was always talking too much. I don't know If I would have been opinionated anyway. I don't know if boarding school makes you <u>resilient</u>. I remember the very first time I read autocue on television. I was quite brilliant at it – and I knew exactly why. We used to have retreats at school which meant two whole days of absolute silence, two days of not speaking unless you absolutely had to. The headmistress knew full well that this was quite impossible for me, so she decided on a policy of damage limitation which was to have me doing something which would stop me disrupting the rest of the school. She made me stand on a chair at the corner of the refectory and read out loud to the whole school at meal times. I do think that if you have ever stood on a chair in front of 200 girls with your green knickers showing, reading out loud from a holy book, nothing truly daunts you again.

There's Something About A Convent Girl

COMPREHENSION

A Choose the best answer for each statement.

1. Anne:
   - **a** wanted to go to boarding school
   - **b** didn't want to go to boarding school
   - **c** had a sister who went to boarding school.

2. She:
   - **a** obeyed the rules
   - **b** got round the rules
   - **c** didn't know the rules.

3. The only letters which the headmistress didn't open were:
   - **a** letters from Ampleforth
   - **b** letters from brothers
   - **c** letters from parents.

4. The headmistress knew that Anne:
   - **a** spoke very little
   - **b** spoke too much
   - **c** didn't say anything.

5. When she had to read an autocue on television, she was:
   - **a** brilliant
   - **b** hopeless
   - **c** daunted.

Unit 5 **Rebel with a cause** / non-fiction

B 1 Explain the following in your own words:
   a *'bucking the system'*
   b *'petty rules'*
   c *'lateral thinking'*.

2 What do you think the writer means when she says *'I never went through a religious period'*?

3 After her experience at the retreat, why do you think nothing daunted her again?

4 How do you know that the headmistress knew Anne's character very well?

C Use evidence from the passage to explain:
   • what sort of person you think Anne is
   • what sort of person you think the headmistress is.

VOCABULARY

Use a dictionary and the context of the passage to explain the meaning of the following words. They are underlined in the passage. The first one is done for you.

1 devious = *cunning* **2** inexplicable

3 credibility **4** liberal

5 opinionated **6** resilient

SPELLING

Double 'm' words

Key word: i**mm**ediately

1 Use the key word above in a sentence of your own.

2 Learn these important **double 'm'** words:

co**mm**a	gra**mm**ar
co**mm**andment	ma**mm**al
co**mm**unication	sy**mm**etry

> **HINT**
> When you add the prefix 'im' to a word beginning with 'm' you will have a word with double 'm', eg *modest – immodest*

90

Something About A Convent Girl

Activity / **5.3**

GRAMMAR AND PUNCTUATION

Apostrophes

> Use the **apostrophe** with contractions, putting it in place of the missing letter or letters,
>
> eg *I **do not** know if boarding school makes you resilient.*
> *'I **don't** know if boarding school makes you resilient.'*
>
> '**don't**' is a contraction.

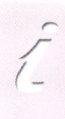

A Copy these sentences. Replace the underlined words with contractions. The first one is done for you.

1 There is always a way round everything.   *There's always a way round everything.*
2 I had fallen deeply in love with a boy at my brother's school.
3 We were not supposed to speak during a retreat.
4 I am still very opinionated.
5 It is very daunting to have to read aloud to so many people.

> Use an **apostrophe** before the 's' to show possession by one person or thing,
>
> eg *the school of my brother   my **brother's** school*

B Copy and complete these sentences, placing apostrophes where they are needed. The first one is done for you.

1 The schools headmistress was Mother Rosemary Alexander.
  The school's headmistress was Mother Rosemary Alexander.
2 The terms highlight was a letter from my boyfriend.
3 The letters content was quite innocent.
4 The schools rules were really petty.
5 The refectorys chairs were very wobbly.

> Use the **apostrophe** after the 's' to show possession by more than one person or thing,
>
> eg *the meal of the pupils   **the pupils' meal***

C Put the apostrophes in the correct place to show these plural owners.

1 my parents envelopes
2 the peoples expectations
3 the teachers decisions
4 the brothers books

Unit 5 Rebel with a cause / non-fiction

Something About A Convent Girl

Activity / 5.3

WRITING

Autobiography

> The editors of *There's Something About A Convent Girl* spoke to famous women who had been to boarding school where their teachers were nuns. They wanted the women to write short, **autobiographical** pieces to explain what they thought of this type of education.

Language features

The writer's attitude

Most of the women explain how they ended up at a convent boarding school,

    eg *'I always wanted to go to boarding school'*

and what they thought of it,

    eg *'it didn't really live up to my expectations'*

The first person

Usually, beginning lots of sentences with 'I' can be boring but the editors wanted a very personal, honest account of what the experience was like,

    eg *'I learnt very little during my time there'* *'I never went through a religious period.'*

Information

Anne Robinson informs the reader of what it was like,

    eg *'convent life was made up, for the large part, of a lot of inexplicable, petty rules.'*

Opinion

The point of putting this book together was to find out what the women thought about their experiences, so the writers include their opinions,

    eg *'They seemed to me to be petty rules'*

       'I was blowed if I wanted Mother Rosemary Alexander to have a look at his letters first.'

Writing assignment

Ask two people (your friends or members of your family) to tell you about an incident they can remember at school. It could be one they found uncomfortable, funny or very serious. Ask questions and take notes about:

- what happened
- how they felt
- what they learnt.

Write up the two incidents in the first person as if the people were writing it themselves.

Show your first draft to the two people to make sure you have written up what they have told you accurately.

Unit 6   What if …? / non-fiction

Cruel Communists…

All men are equal ...

Extract / **6.1**

The idea of 'communism' is a pretty attractive one. 'Everyone is equal. Everything is shared.' The only thing that stops it working is that communists are human beings. And human beings always like to think they're a little better than anyone else ... and too many humans don't like sharing what they've got.

So a communist state has to force people to be equal and to share and then it's not really communist at all – the <u>bullies</u> who do the forcing have power over the weak ones who are forced. You see the problem?

But that didn't stop millions of people in the twentieth century trying to live the communist way – and dying a cruelly communist way too.

- In 1905 the Russian Tsar Nicholas promises to give power to the people in a parliament – then breaks his promise. Sailors who believe in communism <u>rebel</u> and throw their officers overboard. (This is cruel because it's very hard climbing back on board a battleship.) Some of the Tsar's officials are murdered but he survives.
- In 1906 a parliament is formed but has very little power. (The Tsar thinks he's been clever, but if brains were gunpowder he wouldn't have enough to blow his hat off.) The army <u>assassinate</u> a general, but the Tsar survives.
- In 1914 Russia joins the First World War against Germany and suffers terrible defeats. Now the <u>Revolutionaries</u> want peace with Germany but the Tsar won't give in. In fact he says that he'll lead the army himself. So, when it is defeated yet again, the Tsar gets the blame. This time he doesn't survive.
- In March 1917 the Tsar gives up the throne and parliament runs the country and the war. But that's not the real Russian Revolution. A group of communists calling themselves Bolsheviks, led by Trotsky and Lenin, still want peace and tell the soldiers to <u>disobey</u> parliament. The people are starving – 'The Bolsheviks have to be better than this!' they think.
- In November 1917 the Bolsheviks take over Russia. The Communist Revolution has put the Bolsheviks in power, but of course they just spoil the party by <u>squabbling</u> amongst themselves. Millions will die ... including many of the leaders themselves ... in the next 80 years.

Rowdy Revolutions by Terry Deary

COMPREHENSION

A Copy these sentences. Fill in the missing words.

1. Most humans do not like _ _ _ _ _ _ _ what they've got.
2. People who force other people to do things are _ _ _ _ _ _ _.
3. In 1905, the Russian Tsar _ _ _ _ _ _ _ _ promised to give power to the people.
4. The Tsar gave up the throne in _ _ _ _ _, 1917.
5. A group of communists called _ _ _ _ _ _ _ _ _ _ take over Russia.

95

Unit 6 What if ...? / non-fiction

B 1 Explain the following in your own words:
   a *'Everyone is equal'*
   b *'breaks his promise'*
   c *'terrible defeats'*.

2 What, according to the writer, is the basic problem with the idea of communism?

3 In a communist state, what will the bullies do?

4 What do you think is the writer's attitude to the fact that the Tsar seems to survive for so long?

C Find and quote two examples of the writer using humour.

VOCABULARY

Use a dictionary and the context of the extract to explain the meaning of the following words. They are underlined in the passage. The first one is done for you.

1 bullies = *people who force others to do things*
2 rebel
3 assassinate
4 revolutionaries
5 disobey
6 squabbling

SPELLING

Words ending in 'ive'

Key word: attract**ive**

1 Use the key word above in a sentence of your own.

2 Learn these important **'ive'** words:

- act**ive**
- narrat**ive**
- mot**ive**
- negat**ive**
- interact**ive**
- posit**ive**

HINT
Make sure you know the meaning of each word. Use a dictionary.

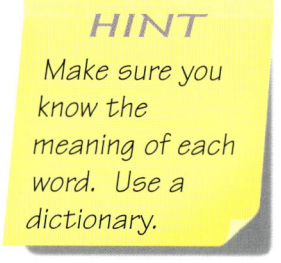

All men are equal ...

Activity / **6.1**

GRAMMAR AND PUNCTUATION

Presentational devices – bullet points / ordering

> **Bullet points** draw attention to important information.
> They stand out on the page and make it easy to find information.
> If you have a group of related items that are not in order, use bullet points.
> This tells the reader that all of the bulleted items are of equal importance.
>
> **Numbers** (1, 2, 3) or **letters** (a, b, c) should be used when things have to be done in a particular order. This tells your reader that number 1 has to be done before number 2 and so on.

Copy the lists below and add:

- bullet points if all the items are of equal importance
- numbers or letters if the items should appear in a particular order.

List 1: Jobs to be done:

Feed the cat
Do the shopping
Wash the car
Buy stamps at the post office

List 2: In order to sell our house, we must:

Install new gutters
Paint the kitchen
Interview at least three estate agents
Select an estate agent
Determine the listing price

List 3: To cut expenses on our next holiday to London:

Check internet sites for cheap hotel accommodation
Book in advance or buy standby tickets for West End shows
Book our flight to Stansted airport instead of Heathrow
Use the Underground instead of taxis

Unit 6 What if ...? / non-fiction

All men are equal ...

Activity / **6.1**

WRITING

Fact and opinion

> The extract from 'Cruel Communists' looks back on how successful or unsuccessful communism was.
> The writer gives:
> - his **opinion** as to why it didn't work
> - **facts** to support his opinion.

Language features

Facts

The writer has researched his subject and presents the facts,
  eg *'In 1906 a parliament is formed but has very little power.'*
      '... Bolsheviks, led by Trotsky and Lenin ...'

Opinion

The writer makes it very clear what his opinion is,
  eg *'The only thing that stops it working is that communists are human beings.'*
      '... too many humans don't like sharing what they've got ...'

Humour

The writer has decided to use humour to entertain the reader,
  eg *'This is cruel because it's very hard climbing back on board a battleship.'*

Writing assignment

Imagine these are a set of rules that the head teacher has written.

1. You must share your pens, pencils, etc with anyone who has forgotten theirs.
2. If someone has not done their homework, you must let them copy yours.
3. You must always be last in the dinner queue.

After six weeks, have these rules worked?

Write a report about:
- the facts – what have you seen happening as people try to obey these rules or disobey these rules?
- your opinion – does it seem to you that these rules work?

Make your report as humorous as possible.

Unit 6 What if …? / non-fiction

…aliens and their spacecraft…

The site of Nellis Airforce Base can be found near the small town of Rachel in the state of Nevada, USA. The Base is a top secret <u>facility</u> where technology for space travel is developed. Part of the Base is known as Area 51. This is even more 'top-secret' and it is said that it houses the remains of two space aliens and their spacecraft.

Area 51 – not of this earth

Extract / **6.2**

The people in Rachel are in no hurry to say that this isn't true! The possibility of captured aliens brings thousands of visitors to this desert spot.

"Everyone in this town has a story," says Brian Paschal, a supposed 'alien expert' who often visits Rachel. "And they're all very suspicious – it's like the moment you step into town, everyone knows about it. You walk into a restaurant, and everyone stops what they're doing and turns around to check you out. It's not hard to feel like an outsider."

"I think there are people and machines from other planets over there," says Pat Travis, co-owner of the Little A'Le'Inn. "And I think our government is working in conjunction with them."

Pat and Joe Travis bought the Rachel Bar and Grill, in 1989 and changed its name to the Little A'Le'Inn. They made the tiny restaurant into a sort of museum and gathering place for anyone interested in aliens. As well as serving food, they also sell alien memorabilia – stickers, hats, T-shirts, posters and stuffed animals. On the walls there are framed photos of UFO sightings from all over the world.

All sorts of visitors come to the restaurant. Some are just curious; some say they have been abducted by aliens; and some say they work for the government.

So, do the people in Rachel really believe in the alien story? After spending some time there, the answer has to be 'yes'. It's not just the Base which convinces them but other odd happenings. Often, strange lights and loud roars are witnessed in the dead of night. One story tells of two women who visited Rachel to investigate UFO rumours. They set out one day, heading for the nearby mountain ranges, and were never seen again.

Glen Campbell, however, is not a believer. He has written an unofficial guidebook of the area in which he describes the entrance to the Base: "The boundaries of the Base are marked by bright orange posts. Do not pass them." He also describes the men who will greet you there, known as 'Cammo dudes'. They are said to watch you from a distance and it is wise at this point to turn the car around and depart. If you pass the orange posts, Campbell claims, you will either be arrested, shot or will vanish without trace.

The government has always denied that there is anything unusual happening in Area 51. Is it just rumour which the locals support because of a thriving tourist trade or have the aliens really landed?

COMPREHENSION

A Write 'true' or 'false' for each of these statements.
1 Nellis Airforce Base is in Nevada.
2 No one in the nearby town of Rachel believes the alien stories.
3 Many tourists come to the town because of the alien stories.
4 Glen Campbell owns the Little A'Le'Inn.
5 The government says that nothing unusual is happening at the Base.

Unit 6 What if ...? / non-fiction

B 1 Explain the following in your own words:
  a *'feel like an outsider'*
  b *'unofficial guidebook'*
  c *'vanish without trace'*.

2 Why do you think the people who live in Rachel *'are in no hurry'* to say the alien stories are not true?

3 Why do you think the Travises changed the name of the restaurant to the 'Little A'Le'Inn'?

4 Why do you think the writer visited Rachel?

C Write a paragraph to explain what the writer thinks about Area 51. Look at:
  - the attitude of the people who live in Rachel
  - the strange happenings
  - the unofficial guidebook.

VOCABULARY

Use a dictionary and the context of the extract to explain the meaning of the following words. They are underlined in the passage. The first one is done for you.

1 facility = *establishment* **2** conjunction

3 memorabilia **4** abducted

5 boundaries **6** depart

SPELLING

Words ending in 'ious'

Key word: suspic**ious**

1 Use the key word above in a sentence of your own.

2 Learn these important **'ious'** words:

anx**ious**   relig**ious**

consc**ious**   ser**ious**

obv**ious**   victor**ious**

HINT
Be careful not to confuse 'ious' endings with 'eous' endings. Use a dictionary to check your spelling.

102

Area 51 – not of this earth

Activity / **6.2**

GRAMMAR AND PUNCTUATION

Punctuation

> Here are the main **punctuation marks** you will need for your writing.
> - full stop **.** at the end of a sentence
>   - eg 'Part of the Base is known as Area 51.'
> - question mark **?** at the end of a question
>   - eg 'So, do the people in Rachel really believe in the alien story?'
> - exclamation mark **!** at the end of a sentence which expresses a humorous point
>   - eg 'The people in Rachel are in no hurry to say that this isn't true!'
> - comma **,** to separate items in a list
>   - eg '... stickers, hats, T-shirts, posters and stuffed animals'
> - to separate clauses
>   - eg 'If you pass the orange posts, Campbell claims, you will either be arrested, shot or will vanish without trace.'
> - speech marks **" "** to show spoken words
>   - eg '"Everyone in this town has a story," says Brian Paschal.'
> - quotation marks **' '** to show you are using someone else's words
>   - eg 'Glen Campbell, however, is not a believer.'

Copy these sentences and punctuate them.

1. I booked a room at the Little A'Le'Inn just for one night
2. What is really happening at Nellis Airforce Base
3. The newspaper reported People claim they have seen strange lights and heard noises in the night
4. When people visit Rachel they find it hard not to believe in the alien story
5. I really believe that there are aliens in there said one visitor
6. The story about the two women who disappeared is frightening
7. I bought a T-shirt poster and the unofficial guidebook
8. Why do you think the government denies anything strange is happening
9. After I'd seen Rachel I was glad I didn't live there
10. The unofficial guidebook warns you that The boundaries of the Base are marked by bright orange posts

Unit 6 What if ...? / non-fiction

Area 51 - not of this earth

Activity / **6.2**

WRITING

Presenting a balanced argument

> The writer of 'Area 51' has set out to look at the evidence concerning the alleged aliens. Are there two sides to the **argument**? Is there really something in the stories or is it just a way for the people of Rachel to make money out of tourists?

Language features

Information
The writer cannot assume the reader knows the facts of what he / she is writing about, so some factual information is necessary,

   eg   '... the Travises renamed the establishment the little A'Le'Inn.'
        'The women were never seen again.'

Setting the tone
The writer creates a serious sense of mystery with descriptions of the area:
>'Often, strange lights and loud roars are witnessed in the dead of night.'
>'They are said to watch you from a distance'

What do people think?
The writer has used the opinions of the people of Rachel:
>' "I think there are people and machines from other planets over there ..." '
>'Glen Campbell, however, is not a believer.'

He also explains how the government's 'opinion' added to the mystery:
>'The government has always denied that there is anything unusual happening in Area 51.'

Writing assignment

Write an article on the subject of a derelict house in your area being haunted. You neither believe nor disbelieve the ghostly stories but want to set out the arguments for and against in an entertaining way. Include:

- comments from people who live in the area
- what you see when you visit the house
- a vivid description of the area and the house.

Think carefully about:

- why some people want to deny the existence of a ghost
- why it would be to some people's advantage to make others believe in the ghost.

105

Unit 6 What if ...? / non-fiction

Found: Key to Jurassic life

DNA clues discovered in 70m-year-old dinosaur – just like in the blockbuster film

Scientists have <u>ventured</u> into the world of Jurassic Park fiction after <u>extracting</u> what look like blood vessels and cells from a fossilised tyrannosaurus rex, it was disclosed yesterday.

They have not ruled out obtaining dinosaur DNA from the samples which are 70 million years old.

Until now the idea of DNA being preserved in ancient dinosaur fossils has not been taken seriously.

But it formed the basis of Michael Crichton's novel *Jurassic Park* which was made into a smash-hit movie by Steven Spielberg. In the film, scientists <u>resurrected</u> terrifying dinosaurs from their DNA. The current research in the United States follows the discovery of a well-preserved tyrannosaurus rex fossil skeleton which was unearthed in 2003 from a site in Montana.

Found: Key to Jurassic life

Extract / 6.3

Scientists examined one of the creature's thigh bones and noticed unusual features in the marrow cavity. Dissolving the fossil mineral deposits with acid left a flexible, stretchy material threaded with what appeared to be transparent and hollow blood vessels.

The vessels branched just like real blood vessels, and some contained cell-like structures.

Dr Mary Schweitzer, from North Carolina State University in Raleigh, in the US, who led the team, told the journal *Science*: "It was totally surprising. I didn't believe it until we'd done it 17 times."

The vessels closely resembled those from the bones of present-day ostriches, the scientist said. Many contained red and brown structures that resembled cells. And within these were smaller objects similar to the structure of blood cells in modern birds.

Using the same technique, scientists isolated similar vessels from another tyrannosaurus rex skeleton and a hadrosaur, a different dinosaur species.

US palaeontologist Dr Lawrence Witmer told *Science*: "If we have tissues that are not fossilised, then we can potentially extract DNA. It's very exciting."

Fossils form after animals are quickly buried in mud or sand, preserving parts of their bodies. Over a long period of time, the tissue is replaced by minerals, forming a rock-like copy of the original object.

If the tyrannosaurus rex tissue is found to contain original material it might open up new ways to study their biochemistry.

Geoff Marsh in *The Daily Express*,
25 March 2005

Jurassic Park   1992   Director: Steven Spielberg
Having found samples of dinosaur DNA, John Hammond sets about creating a dinosaur theme-park on a remote island. The first visitors, however, spend most of their stay on the island, not looking at dinosaurs but being hunted by them! With the advances in film technology, the realism of the dinosaurs is astounding and terrifying!

COMPREHENSION

A Choose the best answer for each statement.

1. Steven Spielberg's film is called:
   a *Science*   b *DNA*   c *Jurassic Park*.

2. The tyrannosaurus rex skeleton was found in:
   a Montana   b North Carolina   c Raleigh.

3. The vessels contained:
   a mud   b DNA   c cell-like structures.

4. Dr Witmer is:
   a a film maker   b a palaeontologist   c a novelist.

5. Animals are fossilised after being:
   a quickly unearthed   b quickly buried   c quickly killed.

Unit 6 What if ...? / non-fiction

B 1 Explain in your own words:
  a *'have not ruled out'*
  b *'not been taken seriously'*
  c *'closely resembled'*.

2 Why do you think the scientists did the experiment *'17 times'*?

3 How do you think Dr Witmer feels about the discovery?

4 Why is it possible that dinosaurs are the ancient ancestors of modern birds?

C Look through the newspaper article carefully and find:

  1 a piece of information

  2 an explanation of how something happens.

VOCABULARY

Use a dictionary and the context of the extract to explain the meaning of the following words. They are underlined in the passage. The first one is done for you.

1 ventured = *gone into*
2 extracting
3 resurrected
4 isolated
5 palaeontologist
6 preserving

SPELLING

Words ending in 'ism'

Key word: real**ism**

1 Use the key word above in a sentence of your own.

2 Learn these important 'ism' words:

- bapt**ism**
- organ**ism**
- Buddh**ism**
- rac**ism**
- hero**ism**
- tour**ism**

HINT
Make sure you know the meaning of each word. Use a dictionary.

Found: Key to Jurassic life

Activity / **6.3**

GRAMMAR AND PUNCTUATION

Quotation marks

> **Quotation marks** " " are used to show direct quotations.
> - You may be quoting what someone actually said,
>   eg *Dr Mary Schweitzer said: "It was totally surprising."*
>
> **Remember!** A colon is used to introduce the quote.

A Copy the sentences and add the quotation marks. The first one has been done for you.

1 One scientist claimed that This is an amazing discovery.

   One scientist claimed that: "This is an amazing discovery."

2 The reporter at *Science* magazine said It was a very interesting story.

3 One person who read the article said It's rubbish. It will never happen.

4 Dr Schweitzer said I work at North Carolina State University.

5 Dr Witmer told *Science* magazine I am a palaeontologist.

> **Quotation marks** can also be used when you are quoting from what you have read,
>   eg *The article in the newspaper stated that: "Until now the idea of DNA being preserved in ancient dinosaur fossils has not been taken seriously."*

B Copy the sentences and add the quotation marks. The first one has been done for you.

1 The novel *Jurassic Park* begins The tropical rain fell in drenching sheets, hammering the corrugated roof of the clinic building, roaring down the metal gutters, splashing on the ground in a torrent.

   The novel Jurassic Park begins: "The tropical rain fell in drenching sheets, hammering the corrugated roof of the clinic building, roaring down the metal gutters, splashing on the ground in a torrent."

2 The title of the newspaper article is Found: Key to Jurassic life.

3 The dictionary says a palaeontologist is someone who studies fossils.

4 Scientists claim that the vessels closely resemble those from the bones of present-day ostriches.

5 The newspaper article says that *Jurassic Park* was a smash-hit movie by Steven Spielberg.

Unit 6 What if ...? / non-fiction

Found: Key to Jurassic life

Activity / **6.3**

WRITING

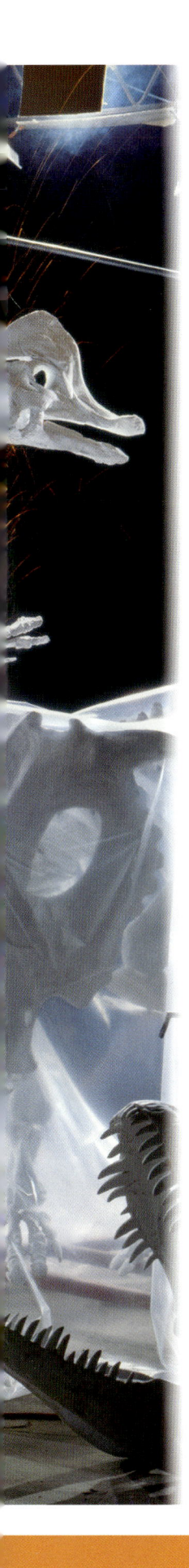

Information and explanation

> The article 'Found: Key to Jurassic life' is written to give the reader:
> - **information**
> - **explanation**.

Language features

Main headline
Newspaper headlines are written to grab the reader's attention. They usually make a dramatic statement and are written in large, bold letters,

eg **Found: Key to Jurassic life**

Smaller headline
Sometimes there is a smaller headline to give the reader more of a clue as to what the article is about,

eg **DNA clues discovered in 70m-year-old dinosaur – just like in the blockbuster film**

Information
Much of the article gives the reader information, eg
- the scientists who are involved: *Dr Schweitzer   Dr Witmer*
- what has been discovered: *'what look like blood vessels and cells from a fossilised tyrannosaurus rex ...'*

Explanation
The article explains some of the technical ideas,

eg *'Fossils form after animals are quickly buried in mud or sand, preserving parts of their bodies.'*

Writing assignment

Imagine you have discovered a dinosaur which no one has ever seen before. It has to have a human feature, eg

> a human voice box which means it could speak   human hands

Write a newspaper article which:
- has an attention-grabbing headline
- informs the reader about where and when it was discovered
- explains to the reader how this discovery changes what we know about dinosaurs.

Text © Wendy Wren 2005

Original illustrations © Nelson Thornes Ltd 2005

The right of Wendy Wren to be identified as author of this work has been asserted by her in accordance with the Copyright, Designs and Patents Act 1988.

All rights reserved. No part of this publication may be reproduced or transmitted in any form or by any means, electronic or mechanical, including photocopy, recording or any information storage and retrieval system, without permission in writing from the publisher or under licence from the Copyright Licensing Agency Limited, of 90 Tottenham Court Road, London W1T 4LP.

Any person who commits any unauthorised act in relation to this publication may be liable to criminal prosecution and civil claims for damages.

Published in 2005 by:
Nelson Thornes Ltd
Delta Place
27 Bath Road
CHELTENHAM
GL53 7TH
United Kingdom

05 06 07 08 09 / 10 9 8 7 6 5 4 3 2 1

A catalogue record for this book is available from the British Library

ISBN 0 7487 9345 3

Illustrations by Mark Berry, Rupert Besley, Ann Biggs c/o Graham-Cameron Illustration, Beverly Curl, Mark Draisy, Jim Eldridge, Paul McCaffrey c/o Sylvie Poggio Artists Agency, Richard Morris, Harry Venning.

Designed by Viners Wood Associates

Printed and bound in Croatia by Zrinski

Acknowledgements
The author and publishers wish to thank the following for permission to use copyright material:

American Legends, Inc for material from the introduction by Ron Martinetti, 'Rebel For All Seasons', to *The James Dean Story* (1995); BBC Worldwide Ltd for an extract from Peter Barnard, *We Interrupt This Programme* (1999) pp. 98-102. Copyright © Peter Barnard 1999; Dorset County Council Youth and Community Service for material from website pages, 'Travelling Abroad' in *Rough Guide to Dorset*, ed. Derek Higton; Express Syndication for extract and photo from Geoff Marsh, 'Found Key to Jurassic life', *Daily Express*, 25.3.05; Hodder and Stoughton Ltd for material from Tanni Grey-Thompson, *Seize the Day* (2001) pp. 22-3; News International Newspapers Ltd for material from Julian Muscat, 'Taylor-made passport to the world', *The Times Davis-Cup Supplement*, 12.7.00. Copyright © Times Newspapers Ltd, London, 2000; Parragon for material from James Weir, *Card Tricks* (1996) pp12-3; Scholastic Ltd for material from Terry Deary, *Horrible Histories Special: Rowdy Revolutions* (1999) pp. 146-7. Copyright © Terry Deary 1999; and Terry Deary, *Horrible Histories: The Vile Victorians* (1994) pp. 44, 46-7. Copyright © Terry Deary 1994; Ed Victor Ltd on behalf of the author for material from Anne Robinsonís contribution to *There's Something About A Convent Girl*, eds. Jackie Bennett and Rosemary Forgan, Virago Press (1991) pp. 155, 157-8. Copyright © 1991 Virago;

Jeff Morgan/Alamy, 86; Bettmann/Corbis, 76, 80; Corel 62 (NT), 32; Corel 161 (NT), 94; Corel 411 (NT), 38; Corel 604 (NT), 32; Corel 640 (NT), 38; Corel 651 (NT), 104; Corel 740 (NT), 44; Bryan Cotton/Assignments Photographers/Corbis, 38; Digital Vision 6 (NT), 26; Digital Vision 11 (NT), 68; Digital Vision 12 (NT), 68; Digital Vision SC (NT), 68; Gerry Ellis/Digital Vision JA (NT), 50; Empics, 64, 70, 74; Cynthia Hart/Corbis, 16; Illustrated London News V1 (NT), 20; Illustrated London News V2 (NT), 20; Image.com/Corbis, 56; Adrian Lee, 52-3; Liverpool Echo/Corbis Sygma, 88; Mark Peterson/Corbis, 100; Photodisc 22 (NT), 32; Photodisc 40 (NT), 44; Photodisc 70 (NT), 44; Photodisc 44 (NT), 50; Louie Psihoyos/Corbis, 110; Roland Grant, 4, 8; Royalty Free/Corbis, 41; Stockpix 7 (NT), 28; Topham Picturepoint, 58.

Every effort has been made to trace the copyright holders but if any have been inadvertently overlooked the publishers will be pleased to make the necessary arrangement at the first opportunity.